Developing Client/Server Applications

D1362201

Computer Books from QED

Developing Client/Server Applications

W. H. Inmon

QED Publishing Group
Boston • Toronto • London

This book is available at a special discount when ordered in bulk quantities. For information, contact Special Sales Department, QED Publishing Group, 170 Linden Street, Wellesley, MA 02181-0013 or phone 617-237-5656.

© 1993 QED Publishing Group
P.O. Box 812070
Wellesley, MA 02181-0013

QED Publishing Group is a division of QED Information Sciences, Inc.

Library of Congress Catalog Number: 93-12201
International Standard Book Number: 0-89435-458-2

Printed in the United States of America
93 94 95 10 9 8 7 6 5 4 3 2

Library of Congress Cataloging-In-Publication Data

Inmon, William H.
    Developing client/server applications / W.H. Inmon.--Rev. ed.
      p.   cm.
    Includes bibliographical references and index.
    ISBN 0-89435-458-2
    1. Client/server computing. I. Title.
QA76.9.C55I55   1993
005.2--dc20
                                                   93-12201
                                                     CIP

Contents

Preface

A doctor can bury his mistakes, but an architect can only advise his clients to plant vines.

Frank Lloyd Wright

The client/server environment is seductive. Unlike the mainframe environment, the developer has complete control over the development and operational activities that occur in the machine in the client/server environment. Furthermore, the costs associated with hardware, software, and networks are so small (relative to other forms of processing) that a devil-may-care attitude pervades client/server processing. Because the developer has complete control over the processor and the costs of development and operations, it is easy to take a relaxed approach to the development process. The systems built for the client/server environment are often built in a lackadaisical, off-hand fashion. But such an attitude toward development is patently dangerous. The size and scale of the environment and the opportunity to control all aspects of operations belie the mess that can be made. Simply stated, unless guided by architectural principles, designers in an autonomous environment such as the client/server world will create chaos. The larger the environment grows, the more chaotic it gets. Just as development in the mainframe environment is structured under a set of guidelines and principles, so the client/server environment should be governed. At least the client/server environment *ought* to be governed by underlying principles.

This book is about those underlying foundations that shape the client/server environment—what they are, how they are implemented, and what happens if they are ignored. Together those principles form an architecture that applies generically across all client/server environments. This book is *not* about any specific client/server technology. Instead, the principles discussed and the resulting architecture that is described apply to *all* technologies that support client/server processing.

The intent of this book is to arm the reader with practical solutions. Very little in the way of theory is presented. Upon reading this book, the reader will be prepared to build very sound, very stable client/server applications. Some of the germane topics to be discussed include

- performance in the client/server environment,
- control of update/"ownership"—"stewardship" of client/server data,
- the difference between operational and DSS processing in the client/server environment,
- application-by-application development versus integration,
- client/server processing and the data warehouse,

- metadata across the client/server environment,
- "requirements-driven development" versus "data-driven development" in the client/server environment,
- DSS processing in the client/server environment, and much more.

This book is for developers, programmers, database designers, managers, database administrators, data administrators, and designers. Students of computer science should also find this book to be of interest.

The author would like to express thanks to the following people for their support throughout this project:

Sheryl Larsen, Platinum Technology
Mark Gordon, Knowledgeware
Cheryl Estep, Chevron
Gary Noble, EPNG
Bill Pomeroy, AGS Consulting
Patti Mann, AMS
Claudia Imhoff, Connect
John Zachman, independent consultant
Sue Osterfelt, Storagetek
Ed Young, Prism Solutions
Ed Berkowitz, attorney/systems analyst

In addition, thanks to Melba Novak for her back-office support.

WHI

Architecture in the Client/Server Environment

Always design a thing by considering it in its next
larger context—a chair in a room, a room in a house,
a house in an environment, an environment in a city
plan.

Eero Saarinen

A working man's definition of architecture is not having
to tear up the street when the power lines are being laid.
Architected properly, the power lines are laid first, then
the street is built. Preparing for all major requirements,
then building the structure in a sequence so that the parts
fit together in a nondisruptive fashion is a good working
definition of architecture.

   Architecture in the client/server world is best understood in terms of a negative example, when things are not
built in a nondisruptive fashion. Consider the following

sequence of events, which are entirely possible in the client/server environment:

1. A small program is built to service an auto parts "on-board" database on one node of the client/server environment.
2. The database is redesigned to include foreign auto parts as well as domestic auto parts.
3. Code is reconstructed to allow update to the database, as well as loading/access of the database.
4. Data is added to show flow of parts—transactions—as well as parts on board.
5. Code is changed and data is altered once again to allow requests to come from a client through the server.
6. In order to determine who can change data, code is added and data is changed to implement an "update control" feature, and so on.

After a few iterations of change to code and data, the system turns into a mess. By not anticipating requirements—by taking the stance that the system was simple and adding complexities incrementally—the developer has produced a maintenance and operational nightmare. Just because client/server systems are smaller than their mainframe cousins does not mean that they are any easier to build or maintain. In some regards client/server systems are more complex than their mainframe cousins. In the mainframe environment, for all its costs and complexities, there are certain basic services done automatically that have to be done individually in the client/server environment. For these reasons then, it is very important to take an architected approach to client/server processing and development. What then, are the shaping factors of a client/server architecture?

1. technology
   - the processors in the network
   - data in the network
   - the network itself
   - programs—systems and applications
2. costs
3. usage
   - DSS processing and operational processing
4. autonomy vs. integration.
5. organizational dynamics
6. structure of data

CLIENT/SERVER PROCESSING—THE BASICS

In its simplest form, a client/server architecture can be depicted as shown in Figure 1.1.

Figure 1.1 shows that there is a network connecting two pc's or workstations (called "nodes" in the network). Other pc's or workstations (i.e., nodes) most certainly will be connected by means of the network, although they are not shown in the simple picture depicted by Figure 1.1. The two pc's in the figure have a special relationship. Pc-B holds and manages data that can be accessed by Pc-A

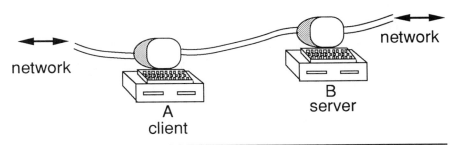

Figure 1.1   A simple perspective of the client/server environment.

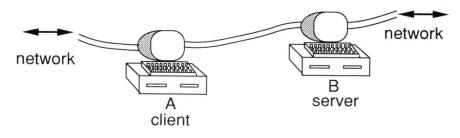

Figure 1.2   The different nodes of the network can be comprised of very different processors, such as pc's and workstations.

through the control of Pc-B. Pc-A is said to be the "client" and Pc-B is said to be the "server." In other words, Pc-B serves the needs of Pc-A. This simple configuration belies the complexity of the applications that are built in a client/server architecture. From a technical standpoint alone, there are many variations of the simple architecture shown in Figure 1.1. For example, Figure 1.2 shows a pc and a larger workstation linked together.

But disparity of processing size among nodes is not the only variable; another important variable is the network itself. Figure 1.3 shows an intermittent linkage between two nodes in the network.

A network may also be connected to another network, as shown by Figure 1.4.

The nodes of a network are organized into "rings." The ring consists of nodes that share the same network. Figure 1.5 shows a ring.

The speed of movement of data within a ring (under normal circumstances) is measured in terms of milliseconds.

Rings are connected to other rings by means of bridges. A bridge is nothing more than a device that controls the traffic from one ring to another. Figure 1.6 shows a bridge.

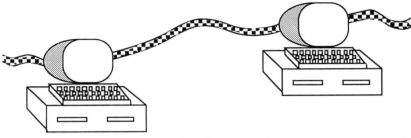

an intermittent linkage between nodes

Figure 1.3	Not only can the technologies found at the nodes vary, but the technology itself may be based on a variety of technologies as well.

There are, then, *many* possibilities in the arrangement of nodes and networks in the client/server environment. But the major issue of client/server architecture does not center around the physical configuration of the nodes and the network. Instead, the major issues of client/server architecture center around the processing that occurs within the architecture and the data stored in and flowing

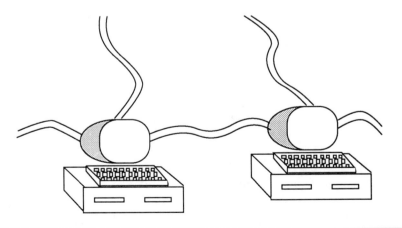

Figure 1.4	Multiply connected nodes to different networks.

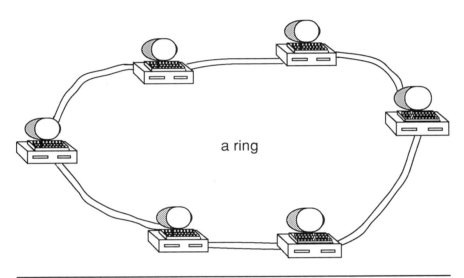

Figure 1.5   A "ring."

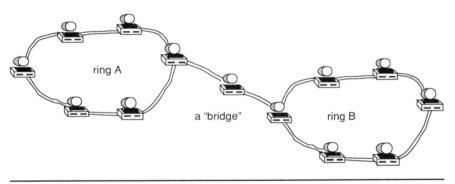

Figure 1.6   A bridge between rings A and B.

through the network itself. Focusing on the technology making up the client/server environment is an interesting thing to do. Certainly the developer/designer needs to be thoroughly grounded in the technology that the client/server environment will run on. But the proper focus of

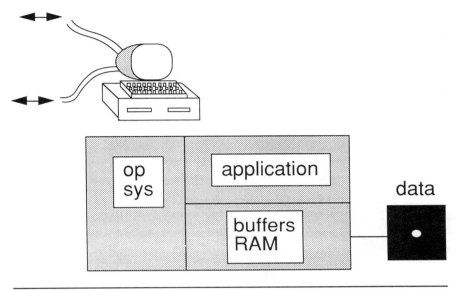

Figure 1.7   The components of each node in the network.

the developer should be not on technology, but on the application(s) being built and the larger structure of processing and data.

A simple arrangement of the important software components found within each node of the network is shown by Figure 1.7. Figure 1.7 shows that each node has an operating system, application programs, internal data, and external data. The external data may be on a wide variety of media, such as tape, floppy disk, etc. (The symbol for floppy disk will be used to represent *all* external media for data storage.) Each node is connected with other nodes by means of the network. Internodal communication is achieved by means of a layered protocol of packets of data. Some nodes have more powerful software components of one or more of these aspects than other nodes. But all nodes share these common characteristics.

One of the interesting questions is how does the client/

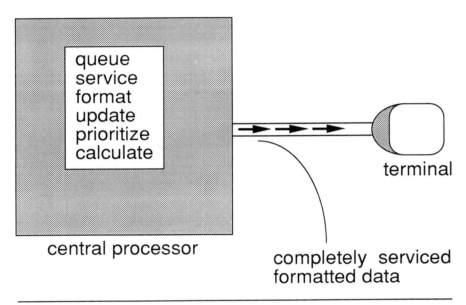

Figure 1.8 A classical centralized architecture.

server architecture differ from classical centralized, mainframe architectures? After all, centralized mainframe architectures existed long before there was client/server processing. Figure 1.8 shows a classical centralized mainframe architecture from the perspective of the receiving terminal. There is an absolute minimum of work done at the terminal. The display of prefabricated, preformatted data and the preformatted collection of data is about all that occurs in a centralized mainframe architecture at the terminal.

Contrast Figure 1.8 with the client/server architecture shown in Figure 1.9.

In Figure 1.9 raw data is passed to a node. Upon arriving at the node, the raw data goes through a series of transformations before being displayed. The raw data can be analyzed and combined with other data at the node. The

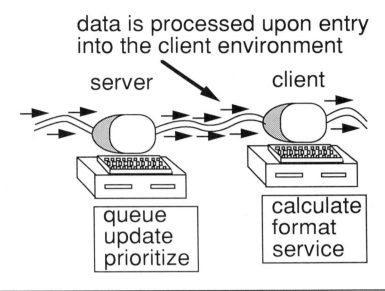

Figure 1.9   Raw data is passed from the server to the client. Much processing can occur at the client processor.

raw data can be formatted in any number of ways prior to display. But the mere receipt of data at a terminal is not the only thing that can be done with data at the client node. Figure 1.10 shows that, unlike data in the mainframe environment, once data arrives at a node in the client/server architecture, it can be recalculated, reformatted, reanalyzed any number of ways, and combined with other data without necessarily returning to the server.

Sometimes the client/server environment is called a "smart" environment because after the delivery of data to the client node, much processing can occur. In the mainframe environment, very little if any processing can occur at the terminal once the data arrives. For this reason the mainframe environment is called a "dumb" environment.

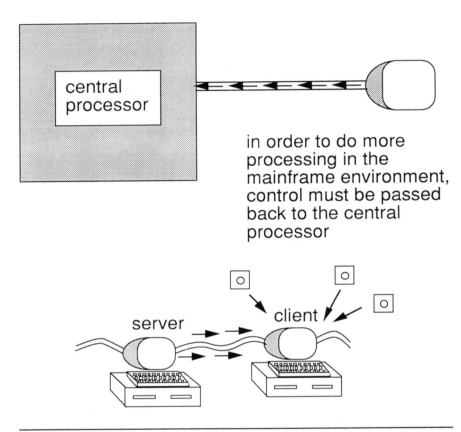

in order to do more processing in the mainframe environment, control must be passed back to the central processor

Figure 1.10   Once data arrives at the client site, it can be processed many times without having to return control to the server.

COSTS

A second shaping factor of the client/server architecture is that of cost. The entire cost scale of client/server processing is lower than the corresponding costs associated with larger mainframe processors. The differences in cost show up in

- processor costs,
- network costs,
- development costs,
- operations costs,
- software system costs, and
- maintenance costs.

Only the last of these costs—maintenance—normally remains (or *can* remain) constant across the client/server and other environments. The reason why client/server maintenance costs can be less than maintenance costs for their larger brethren is because client/server applications usually are smaller and simpler. However, if an architected approach to client/server applications is not taken, maintenance of client/server applications can become as burdensome and costly as maintenance of any other applications in any environment.

USAGE OF THE APPLICATION

The third architectural factor shaping the client/server world is the way in which client/server applications are built, and once built, how these applications are used. The usage of client/server processing can be classified as either operational usage or DSS usage. This difference in usage is perhaps not only the most profound, most important factor in applications development, but also the most misunderstood, most neglected factor there is.

To begin with, what is operational processing? Operational processing is processing that affects the day-to-day detailed business decisions that are made. How much coverage does an insuree have? What was the last payment made to an account? How much is the balance on a loan? Where was the last claim against a policy made by the company? and so forth. Some of the salient characteristics of operational processing are:

- Operational processing operates on current value data—data whose accuracy is current as of the moment of usage.
- Operational development is classically done one application at a time.
- Operational processing is requirements-driven. This means that a set of requirements is laid out a priori and the resulting application is run repetitively.
- Operational processing manipulates—updates or accesses—data on a detailed record-by-record basis.
- Operational processing has access to archival data that has a high probability of access and a relatively low volume.
- The issue of ownership of data—who can update data—is germane to the operational environment.
- Operational processing is for the benefit of the clerical community making up-to-the-second decisions.

DSS processing (i.e., decision support systems processing) is diametrically different from operational processing. DSS processing is used to support the managerial community, not the clerical community. DSS processing has these characteristics:

- DSS processing operates on archival data. Archival data, once recorded properly, is not able to be updated. Archival data is fundamentally different from current value data, which of course can be updated.

- DSS processing is done on integrated data, as opposed to data that is collected one application at a time.
- DSS processing is essentially data-driven; operational processing is requirements-driven.
- DSS processing operates on data on a collective basis, not on a detailed basis.
- DSS processing has access to archival data that has a modest to low probability of access.
- Who can update DSS data is not an issue since DSS data, once written, cannot be updated.
- DSS processing serves the managerial community in the making of long term decisions.

There are, then, very significant differences between operational and DSS processing, as evidenced by these issues. Understanding the differences between operational processing and DSS processing is essential to success in the client/server environment. When the developer does not understand the difference (or even worse, when the developer is not even aware that there is an issue), the result is a very disharmonious client/server environment.

Perhaps the most obvious, most profound difference between operational and DSS processing in the client/server environment lies in how hardware resources are used. Operational and DSS processing display very, very different patterns of hardware utilization. Figure 1.11 shows those patterns of hardware utilization.

Figure 1.11 shows that client/server hardware is used statically—with minor peaks and valleys—in the operational environment. At the end of the day, with operational usage of data, you can calculate the average client/server hardware utilization and have a meaningful number.

The pattern of hardware utilization for DSS processing is fundamentally different. The pattern of DSS pro-

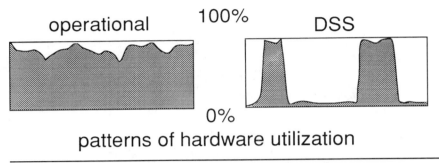

patterns of hardware utilization

Figure 1.11   Operational and DSS processing exhibit very different patterns of hardware utilization.

cessing is a binary pattern. In DSS client/server processing, either the hardware is being heavily used or the hardware is not being used at all. Calculating an arithmetic mean for client/server hardware utilization in the DSS environment results in a meaningless number.

The argument can be made that so little processing is done in the client/server environment relative to the amount of available processing resources that the difference between hardware utilization in the operational and the DSS environment is negligible. It is true that if you are doing only a smidgen of processing and are using 10 percent or less of your total hardware capacity in the client/server network, the profound difference between hardware utilization in operational and DSS processing does not show up.

But such a small hardware utilization figure for the client/server environment is usually economically unfeasible. A serious production application in the client/server environment will use enough resources so that the fundamental resource utilization patterns for the client/server environment become a very important issue. And when hardware utilization rises, the differences between operational and hardware utilization become noticeable and pronounced.

DSS/OPERATIONAL DIFFERENCES AND CLIENT/ SERVER PROCESSING

The differences between operational and DSS processing have a profound effect on the way applications should be built in the client/server environment. Unequivocally, there should be a separation—logical and physical—of operational and DSS processing. Mixing the two types of processing, either inadvertently or consciously, in the face of a serious amount of processing, leads to

* maintenance bottlenecks,
* performance bottlenecks, and
* application complexity.

A good way to separate operational and DSS processing in the client/server environment is to isolate operational processing onto one ring and DSS processing onto another ring.

In short, the very factors that make the client/server environment so attractive in the first place are negated by an unaware designer who freely mixes operational and DSS processing.

AUTONOMY VS. INTEGRATION

Another major architectural factor that shapes the client/ server environment is that of autonomous processing versus integrated, corporate processing. One of the great appeals of the client/server environment is that of autonomy of processing that is afforded by independence at each node. There is independence of processing, independence of data, independence of utilization, and so forth. Once data arrives at a node, the user has control of the data, even in the face of pre-packaged applications. It is no great trick to move data from the pre-packaged application into private files of data resident at the node.

Under all conditions there needs to be some degree of freedom at each node. However, there is a concomitant need for uniformity and consistency of data and processing when the data and/or processing is "corporate" data that happens to reside at the node but is needed across the network. For example, suppose that one node in the network is for the auto insurance actuary. In terms of making private calculations, the actuary uses the node regularly. No one else is concerned with what the actuary does in so far as individual analysis of automobile data is concerned. But when the actuary decides to change corporate rates for auto insurance, including coverages, length of policies, renewal terms, and so forth, the rates have to be changed in a "corporate" manner, so that all affected people across the network know about the change. At each node, there is both private, autonomous data and public, corporate data. Not making the distinction between the two types of data and freely intermixing the data within the node can lead to collective chaos across the client/server environment.

A MATRIX

A matrix can be built in order to classify the different types of client/server applications there are, as shown by Figure 1.12.

A node autonomous application in the client/server environment is one that is wholly self-contained. In other

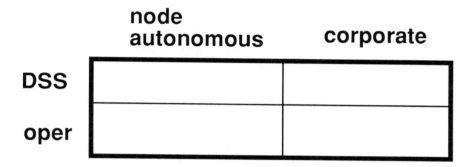

node autonomous corporate

DSS

oper

Figure 1.12 The basic client/server matrix into which all applications may be classified. Note that the characteristics of an application differ widely from the characteristics of another application in another quadrant of the matrix.

words, a node autonomous application has no storing of data or communication with other nodes in the network.

A corporate client/server application is one where multiple nodes work together in an integrated, cooperative manner.

Figure 1.12 shows that client/server applications can be built that are DSS/node autonomous, operational/node autonomous, DSS/corporate, and operational/corporate. While the node autonomous applications—DSS or operational—can be very interesting, the focus of this book is on those "corporate" client/server applications. These applications are of interest because this is where the organization achieves its largest leverage and payback with client/server processing.

ORGANIZATIONAL DYNAMICS

The great appeal of the client/server environment is that the cost of acquiring and operating is within the budget of the department. There no longer is a need for massive corporate mainframe budgets. Concomitant with the control afforded the department, as it becomes the master of its own destiny, is the need to work closely and cooperatively with other departments that likewise have taken control of their own processing.

If each department goes its own way with no concern for the commonality of data and processing that is shared with other departments, the result is institutionalized chaos. There is a certain amount of consistency and uniformity that is desirable across the many departments of a company. The cost of client/server processing and the scale of client/server processing make it easy for the organization to ignore its role as a member of a larger community. There is the very real danger that the result of client/server acceptance is the building of many islands of processing. The lack of integration that results negates many, if not all advantages of going to the client/server environment in the first place.

It is then the responsibility of each organization engaging in client/server processing to recognize and proactively promote its role as an independent member of a community where there is commonality of data and commonality of processing across the organization.

Structure of Data

The structure of data has always been important in all processing environments. It is of even more importance within the client/server environment. The first major division of data structure that is important is within the node itself—what data is public (or corporate), and what data is private must be clearly delineated. Mixing the two types of data within the node is not a good idea.

The second division of data is between the operational

and DSS nodes of the network. There can be no confusion as to how data is aligned.

The third major structuring of data in the client/server environment is that of the organization of archival, DSS data into what is termed the "data warehouse." The data warehouse, in the client/server environment, is the repository of data for DSS processing. The client/server data warehouse is:

- organized along the major "subjects" of the corporation,
- integrated across all client/server applications,
- non-volatile, appearing as a collection of snapshots of data,
- time-variant, where each snapshot of data has its moment of execution recorded.

The data warehouse in the client/server environment can be implemented in any number of ways—over several servers, on a single server, or even residing on a separate network or mainframe computer.

SUMMARY

In this chapter, the importance of architecture has been outlined. Without an architected approach to development in the client/server environment, the advantages of the client/server environment are negated. The factors that shape the architecture of the client/server environment are

- the technology on which client/server systems are run;
- the costs throughout the development life cycle;
- the usage (applications) that is built, specifically including the need to separate operational and DSS data and processing; and
- the need to distinguish between node autonomous processing and "corporate" processing.

2

The Client/Server Environment—Some Issues

The most immutable barrier in nature is between one man's thoughts and another's.

William James

There are several great appeals of the client/server environment: the cost of building systems, the costs of operating systems, and, not the least, the control and autonomy that are afforded both the developer and the user in the client/server environment.

Cost. Simply stated, it is cheaper to develop and operate systems in a client/server environment than it is in other environments.

Control. Because of the small size of the technology found and used in the client/server environment, (primarily pc and workstation technology) there is an air of control that is not present in mainframe software and hardware. The world of mainframe technology is so large, so vast, and so complicated that at best a developer controls only a small piece of turf. The developer in the mainframe environment is helpless to do many activities for himself/herself. Even the user in the mainframe environment feels lost. There are many other users, each with their own agenda, and no two agendas which are the same. The mainframe environment of necessity is run by consensus of opinion. Prioritization of processing, configuration, and even what system software is to be used is a matter of public concern, where the majority rules. It is really easy for a user to get lost in the crowd in the mainframe environment.

The same collective mindset is not found in the client/server environment. Within the bounds of reasonability, each node in the client/server network can be tailored to fit the user and only the user. The express individual needs of the user shape each node. It is this element of individuality and control that make the client/server environment so seductive. But cost and control are not the only issues relevant to client/server processing.

OTHER ISSUES

Performance is the length of time from the moment a user initiates a request until the request has been satisfied and the results are obvious and usable.

Performance is an issue in the client/server environment, although it takes on a somewhat different form than it does in other arenas. Performance begins to be an issue when the client/server applications mature, and the volume of data and the volume of processing running in the client/server environment begin to be noticeable. Performance as an issue often first appears in the flooding of

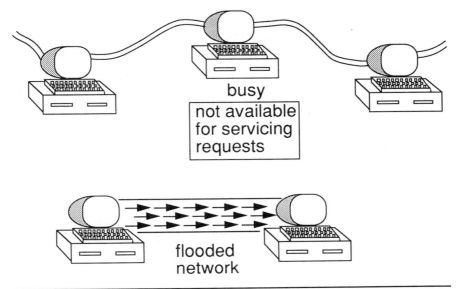

Figure 2.1   Two manifestations of poor performance in the client/server environment.

the network and/or in the case where a node is busy processing one demand and cannot service other requests. There are other manifestations of performance, but these symptoms are usually the first sign of a performance problem.

Another way of looking at performance in the client/server environment is to view performance

- from one node to the next,
- from external storage to internal storage, and
- from internal storage to the screen.

Figure 2.2 shows this perspective of performance in the client/server environment.

The first perspective of performance—of moving data from one node to the next is expressed in units of time from 10 seconds up to 24 hours, depending on the amount of data, the other processing that is occurring, whether the environment is DSS or operational, and so forth. The second perspective of performance—of moving data from external storage to internal storage—is measured in terms of 10's of milliseconds. The third perspective—that of moving data from internal storage to the screen—is measured in terms of fractions of milliseconds.

Uniformity of corporate processing. A second major concern of client/server processing is that of uniformity of corporate processing, i.e., nonautonomous processing. The more autonomy of processing there is, the more the problem of uniformity/consistency becomes an issue. For "corporate" client/server applications, uniformity is a real issue.

Ownership of data. Going hand in hand with the issue of uniformity/consistency of corporate processing is the issue of ownership of data. Who can update data? Who is responsible for updating data? Who should keep data resident at their node? Who can access data? There are many facets to the issue of ownership.

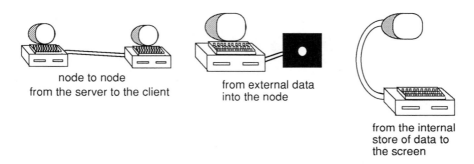

node to node
from the server to the client

from external data
into the node

from the internal
store of data to
the screen

Figure 2.2   Three important perspectives of performance for the client/server environment.

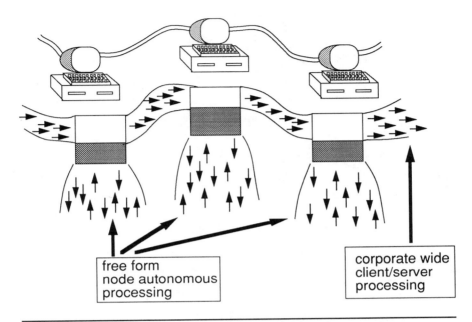

Figure 2.3   The mixture of the different types of processing across the nodes of the client/server network.

Discipline. One approach to the client/server environment is to proclaim pure autonomy at all nodes. This proclamation may have the effect of immediate satisfaction of end user needs. But over the long haul, as the organization matures, it becomes apparent such an approach will not meet the needs of the organization. For those activities and those data that have applicability and use throughout the organization, pure autonomy at each node in the client/ server environment will not suffice. Autonomy across the network at each node for corporate wide data and processing robs the organization of the opportunity for

- integration,
- uniformity, and
- economies of development, maintenance.

And how does a corporation achieve integration across different nodes? Integration is achieved through discipline. Figure 2.3 shows the mixture of pure node autonomous processing and corporate wide processing.

OUTER LIMITS OF REASONABILITY

Any computer environment has its reasonable limits of capacity for processing, and the client/server environment is no exception. Whether capacity is measured in number of users, amount of data, number of programs run, or size of network, there is an upward limit at which point the client/server architecture would best be served by another approach, despite the appealing nature of the client/server environment.

The upward limits of technology are raised each year, as hardware processing capabilities grow and the cost of processors and other hardware drops. But even with this beneficial cost/benefit curve working for the client/server environment, there nevertheless is a technological upper limit at which point the client/server architecture is no longer effective. The technological upper limit is especially applicable to the data warehouse portion of the client/server environment. The designer needs to have a feel for exactly what the limit is, and whether the processes being designed and the stores of data being planned will in fact exceed those limits.

SYSTEM OF RECORD

One cornerstone of client/server applications is the notion of the difference between and separation of operational and DSS processing. Another cornerstone is the difference between "corporate" processing and node autonomous processing. And yet another cornerstone is the concept of the "system of record." The system of record is merely the notion that for all data that can be updated, at any moment in time there is one and only one node that is responsible for update. An essential part of any serious corporate client/server application is the definition of the system of record. The instant that two or more parties (i.e. nodes) have "control"—simultaneous control—over the same piece of data at the same time, there is a fundamental flaw with the system. In order to maintain control and discipline over the nodes in the client/server network, there *must* be defined a "system of record." The system of record can take many different forms. It is not necessary to have a single rigid definition or a single rigid implementation. But it is absolutely necessary to have a definition and understanding of the system of record. Figure 2.5 shows several possibilities for implementations of the system of record.

The importance of establishing the system of record for both the operational and the DSS environment is illustrated by Figure 2.4.

Without a carefully defined system of record, data is scattered across the client/server environment and no one knows what is the right data for operational or for DSS purposes. The client/server environment is peculiarly vulnerable to the phenomena shown in Figure 2.4 because of the autonomy of data and the autonomy of processing at each of the nodes.

In the first simple case shown in Figure 2.5, only a single node can update all policies. Other nodes can request access to a policy and may take policy information to their node, but may not change any information. In the second case, node A can update policies for customers whose names begin with A to M, and node B can update policies for customers where names begin with N to Z.

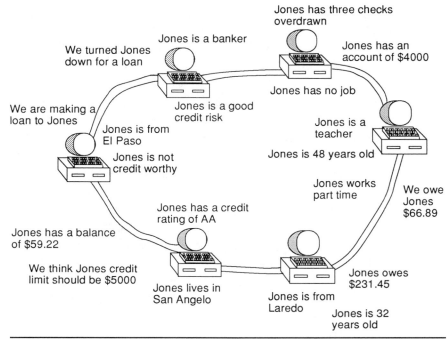

Figure 2.4   A manager's nightmare—what happens when each user at each node "does their own thing."

And in the third case, node A updates all policies, except that on occasion node A "passes" a policy to another node. Then for a specific time for a specific policy, the node that has had the policy passed to it can update the policy and no other node can. Then the updated policy is returned to node A.

In all three of these cases, there is one and only one "owner" or "manager" of data at any moment in time, thus adhering to the system of record. Note that there are many variations to the three simple examples shown in Figure 2.5, although the three options shown are probably the most straightforward and common.

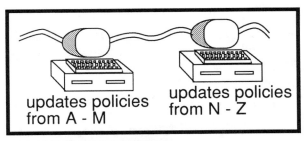

updates policies from A - M

updates policies from N - Z

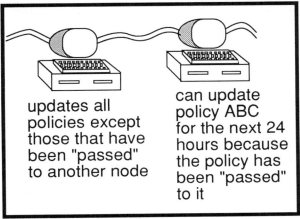

updates all policies except those that have been "passed" to another node

can update policy ABC for the next 24 hours because the policy has been "passed" to it

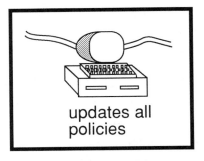

updates all policies

Figure 2.5   The control of update and ownership of data for corporate-wide processing in the client/server environment is very important. Identifying the "system of record" or node residency is one of the most important design issues.

In any case, an operational, corporate client/server application is in real trouble the minute that the system of record is not clearly and accurately defined.

CURRENT VALUE DATA VERSUS ARCHIVAL DATA

The system of record is primarily applicable to current value data. What is current value data? Simply stated, current value data is data that can be updated. Current value data is data whose accuracy is valid as of the moment of access. Operational systems are almost exclusively based on current value data. Some typical operational uses of operational current value data are:

- What is the customer's phone number, right now?
- The customer wants to cash a check. Is there enough money in the customer's account, right now?
- There is not enough money in the customer's account. Does the customer have valid overdraft protection in effect, right now?
- The customer wants to execute a bank card activity. Will the bank card charge put the customer over his/her limit, right now?

In other words, current value data is the reflection of information or status right now. And current value data can change or be updated, on a moment's notice.

Contrast current value information with archival information. Archival data is that older data that has accumulated as a by-product of operational processing. Archival data is often thought of as existing in terms of snapshot. An event occurs that triggers a snapshot of data. The snapshot is made and is stored for posterity. Throughout the history of information processing—long before there were client/server architectures—archival data has been treated as an afterthought. Archival data has been the original Wednesday's child of data processing. And that's too bad because much valuable DSS analysis is based on archival data. It is suggested that those developers of client/server applications not repeat the mistake of their earlier mainframe cousins. Archival data is data whose value is relevant to or accurate as of some moment in time. Once archival data is correctly recorded and stored in a snapshot, it is not ever changed. (On occasion it has been changed—the practice is known as *fraud!*) Archival data in general takes three forms:

- Continuous. From December 1989 to March 1990, customer Jones lived at 123 High Street.
- Event discrete. On May 15, 1991 customer Jones was granted a loan for $2500.
- Periodic discrete. Each month, the credit bureau reports on customer Jones.

Archival data usually exists in large bulk. Relative to current value data, archival data is much more voluminous. The large volume of data found in archival storage poses an especially challenging problem for the client/server designer. The typical PC's and workstations found in the client/server environment are quickly overwhelmed by the volume of data aggregating in the archival store.

Because archival data cannot be updated, the system of record does not apply to it the way the system of record applies to current value data. In other words, from a technical infrastructure perspective, from an application design perspective, from a development perspective, there is a very different treatment of data and processing in regard to the system of record when dealing with archival data and current value data. This fundamental issue is as important to the client/server developer as it is to the developer in any other environment.

NODE RESIDENCY—A MAJOR ISSUE

Another very important design issue in the client/server environment is that of node residency of data and the probability of access of data. The probability of access of data is the primary factor shaping what data resides at what node. As a rule, each node should process data that is most convenient to it. The more often that processes in execution at one node have to rely on data residing at another node, the less efficient (and the more complex) processing becomes. In addition, when there is massive storing of data across nodes, there is a much greater chance that the system of record will become confused or compromised. The net result of positioning data and processing locally at the resident node is a much "cleaner" client/server operating environment. Figure 2.6 shows the difference to the network that is made by satisfying most processing locally, at the resident node.

On the left, processing is done mostly locally, with little or only occasional need to cross the network to get data from another server. On the right, the network is frequently crossed. There are several beneficial effects of minimizing the crossing of the network:

- There is much less network traffic.
- There is the potential for much better performance.
- The server issuing the request may have to go into a "wait state" until the data it needs is returned. When there is not much need to go to another node for data, the processing node has little need to go into a "wait state."

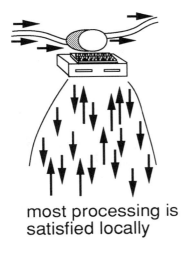

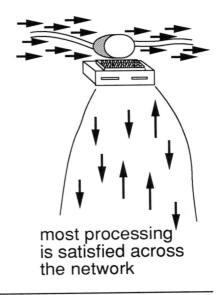

most processing is
satisfied locally

most processing
is satisfied across
the network

Figure 2.6   The difference between local processing and
corporate processing.

Of the two effects, the second is much more important to
overall user satisfaction.

In the ideal state, very little passage of bulks of data
should occur on the network. For example, suppose that
nodes are organized as shown in Figure 2.7.

Here, one node is responsible for accounting, another
node is responsible for marketing, and a third node is responsible for actuarial processing. Such an arrangement
can be called a "functional" assignment of node residency.
It is clear which node is in control of what data based on
the function being serviced.

One of the problems with the configuration shown in
Figure 2.7 is that the same data most likely will be found
in more than one place. For example, the same information about customer Jones would be spread across the
network. This greatly complicates matters even in the

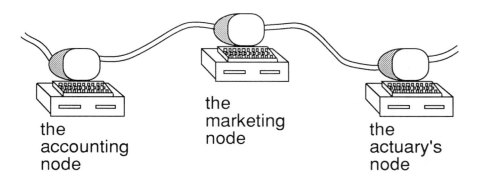

Figure 2.7   A functional delineation of node residency.

face of a carefully defined system of record. Based on the node residency shown in Figure 2.7, the probability of access is not clear.

Another strategy for determining the residency of data at any node is that shown by Figure 2.8.

Figure 2.8 shows that data is split by unique (and hopefully distinct) types of data. In this split of data, one node controls customer information, another node controls account information, and yet a third node controls premium information. There is very little overlap of data in this configuration. The difference between Figures 2.7 and 2.8 is that in Figure 2.7 residency of data is decided by processing, and in Figure 2.8 residency of data at any node is decided by type of data.

In the first case, there is little overlap of processing and much overlap of data. In the second case, there is little overlap of data, and potentially much overlap of processing. It is noted, however, that whatever the advantages or disadvantages, the functional split of node residency is politically and organizationally much more

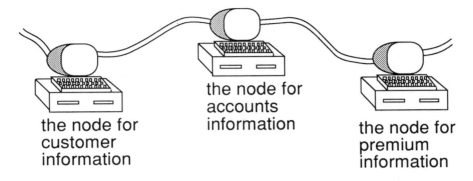

the node for
customer
information

the node for
accounts
information

the node for
premium
information

Figure 2.8   A "data" or "subject" delineation of node residency.

appealing. Figure 2.9 shows the difference between the two strategies.

When the designer chooses to make each node process-based, there will of necessity be much redundancy of data, much sharing of data across the network, and great complexity. When the designer chooses to base node residency on data, the result is limited redundancy of data, simplicity of processing, etc. It is easier to write a program, and execute that program on multiple nodes, than it is to write a program that will run on only one mode and shuffle data throughout the network. However advantageous this option is, it is seldom chosen because of the orientation toward organizational alignment with node residency.

Note that when node residency is data based, there will still be some amount of redundancy of data.

Yet another common arrangement of node residency of data, a geographical orientation, is shown in Figure 2.10.

In Figure 2.10, node residency is divided along lines of geography. One node services Northwest processing, another node services Southeast processing, another node services Northeast processing, and so forth. Data is non-

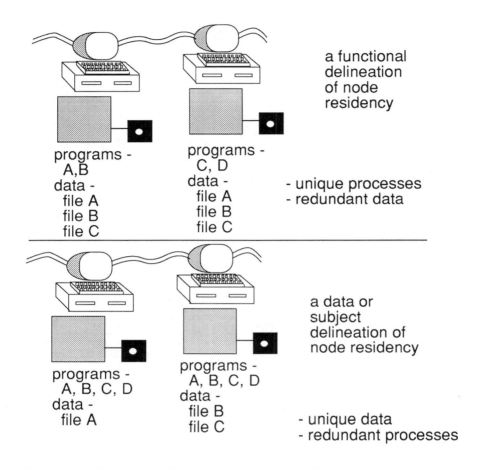

programs -
   A,B
data -
   file A
   file B
   file C

programs -
   C, D
data -
   file A
   file B
   file C

a functional
delineation
of node
residency

- unique processes
- redundant data

programs -
   A, B, C, D
data -
   file A

programs -
   A, B, C, D
data -
   file B
   file C

a data or
subject
delineation of
node residency

- unique data
- redundant processes

Figure 2.9   The trade off between a functional delineation of
                   node residency and a data or subject delineation
                   of node residency.

redundant, for the most part, across the different nodes.
Depending upon where any business occurs or is managed, the business will be directed to one or the other
node. In terms of processing, the same programs are
found across the different nodes. The structure of data,

not the content of data, is spread out across the different nodes. The different possibilities and their relevant tradeoffs (and there are plenty more than shown here) are depicted in Figure 2.11.

Each of the possibilities for node residency has its strengths and weaknesses. In general, it is easy to keep programs and data structure redundant across multiple nodes. It is not easy, even with a well-defined and well-administered system of record, to keep redundant data under control. As a rule, node residency is decided by the orientation of the organization controlling the node. If the

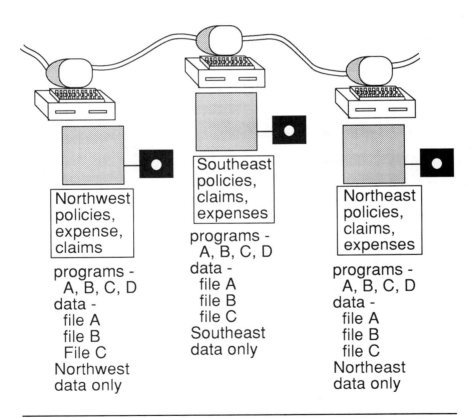

Figure 2.10 A geographical delineation of node residency.

organization has a geographical split across like units, the client/server network will likewise have a geographical delineation of node residency. If the organization has a functional division from other organizations, the client/server network will likewise exhibit a functional split.

The designer is asking for trouble if the delineation of node residency does not fit that of the organization being served by the client/server environment.

Another way to address the issue of node residency is by making a clear separation between nodes that process

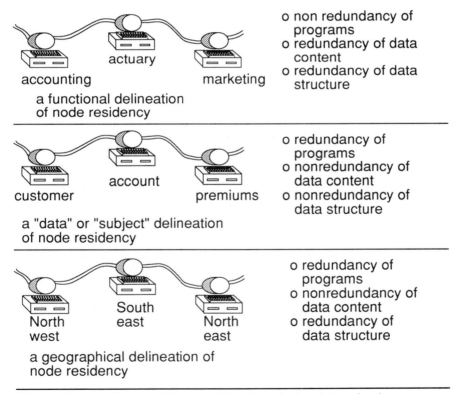

o non redundancy of programs
o redundancy of data content
o redundancy of data structure

accounting   actuary   marketing
a functional delineation of node residency

o redundancy of programs
o nonredundancy of data content
o nonredundancy of data structure

customer   account   premiums
a "data" or "subject" delineation of node residency

o redundancy of programs
o nonredundancy of data content
o redundancy of data structure

North west   South east   North east
a geographical delineation of node residency

Figure 2.11   Some of the considerations in the determination of node residency.

data (i.e., clients), and nodes that hold and manage data exclusively (i.e., servers). In other words, instead of having general purpose nodes that both process data and manage data, a common strategy is to create a division in processors so that any given node is a client or a server.

When clearly delineated, many of the problems of the system of record disappear. For one thing, a server can be large enough to manage enough data to be able to hold enough data for all functions or all subject areas. It is not uncommon to have a server that is of a much larger size than the client workstations or PC's. In addition, the server is free of general purpose duty.

Of course, when data must be spread over multiple servers, the system of record and orientation of the node issues surface.

When data is held at the client for any length of time at all, the issue of the system of record surfaces once again. Even though the data is read from the server and moved to the client, if the client can update the data, then the system of record must be clearly delineated. Figure 2.12

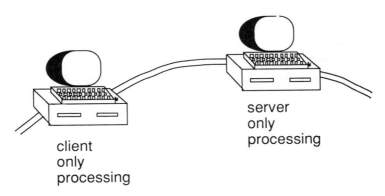

client
only
processing

server
only
processing

Figure 2.12   In this configuration, a server manages data exclusively and a client manages processing exclusively. This can be termed "pure" mode or the "exclusive" mode.

shows the configuration of a "pure" client and a "pure" server environment.

SYSTEM DEVELOPMENT LIFE CYCLE

Another factor profoundly affecting the client/server environment is that of the differences in the system development life cycle (SDLC) between operational and DSS processing. Previously, the differences between the operational and the DSS environment have been discussed in terms of data, resource utilization, and other aspects. Those differences are very important. But there is another very important difference between operational and DSS processing and that difference is in the way systems are developed. The classical approach to systems development is shown by Figure 2.13.

Figure 2.13 shows the classical SDLC and manpower utilization beginning with requirements and ending with implementation and maintenance. The classical SDLC applies only to operational systems. The very nature of DSS processing is heuristic analysis. Heuristic analysis is analysis such that the next step of development is not formulated until the results of the current step of processing are completed. In a word, heuristic processing is iterative.

The way that systems are developed in the DSS mode is almost completely opposite the way systems are developed in the operational mode. For this reason, the system development life cycle for DSS processing is often called the "CLDS" ("SDLC" backwards). Figure 2.14 shows the CLDS for DSS processing.

Progress occurs in an iterative fashion in the client/server DSS environment. First, data—archival, time-variant data—is implemented. Next, the data is tested to determine completeness, bias, etc., and programs are

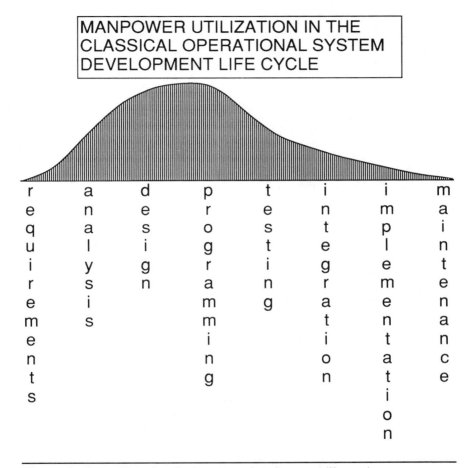

MANPOWER UTILIZATION IN THE CLASSICAL OPERATIONAL SYSTEM DEVELOPMENT LIFE CYCLE

requirements analysis design programming testing integration implementation maintenance

Figure 2.13   The classical system development life cycle (SDLC) along with manpower requirements.

written and run against the data. After running, the results of the program are analyzed. Upon several iterations of the process described, the requirements for DSS processing are finally unmasked.

The DSS environment is typified by the attitude of the end user: "Give me what I say I want; then I will tell you

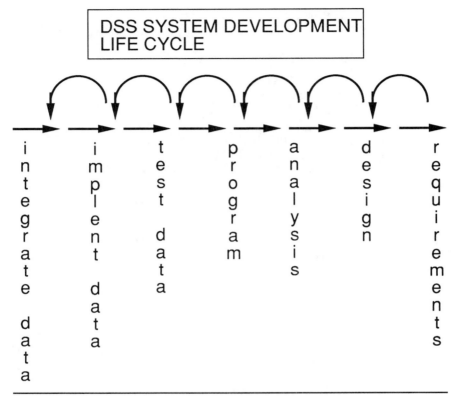

Figure 2.14   The system development life cycle for decision support processing (DSS)—almost a mirror image of the classical SDLC. Note that DSS processing is iterative throughout.

what I really want." The end user operates in a mode of discovery. It is only after seeing a screen or a report that the possibilities become apparent to the end user. Where requirements must be laid in concrete (as in the classical SDLC), the attitude of discovery (which, interestingly, is a perfectly valid attitude), drives classical SDLC developers crazy, because they never complete the requirements gathering process.

As if there were a need for further reason for the separation of operational and DSS processing in the client/server environment, the very, very different patterns of development reinforce the need to separate operational and DSS data and processing.

SUMMARY

In this chapter some of the major issues facing the developer in the client/server environment have been discussed. They are

- the element of control in the client/server environment that is not present in other environments
- performance across the network and at each node
- uniformity of processing
- discipline
- the establishment of the system of record
- current value data versus archival data
- node residency
- system development life cycle

Each of these issues has a profound effect on the way the client/server environment is shaped and on the way applications are developed.

3

The System of Record and Operational/DSS Processing

The secret of business is to know something that nobody else knows.

Ari Onassis (1900–1975)

The establishment and implementation of the system of record form one of the foundations of a successful client/server environment. Interestingly, the system of record takes on very different forms for operational, current value data and for DSS, time-variant data. Both aspects and implementations of the system of record, in the operational and in the DSS environment, will be discussed in this chapter.

THE OPERATIONAL SYSTEM OF RECORD FOR CLIENT/SERVER PROCESSING

The most natural, most normal split of node residency is along the lines of functionality, or along the political divisions, of the organization responsible for the node. (There *are* other approaches toward node residency; the most common approach will be discussed in this chapter.) The reason that node residency is naturally split along functional, or political lines is that the essence of client/server processing is of control and autonomy. It is very natural then for each functional department to control its own node. For an example of a functional, or political, division of node residency, refer to Figure 3.1.

Figure 3.1 depicts node residency for a retail/wholesale grocery distributor. One node is for accounting, another node is for suppliers orders (i.e., order made to a supplier), and yet another node is for docking processing, where shipments are made and received. For the most part, there is a fair amount of unique, nonoverlapping processing in each of the nodes, as well as a fair amount of overlap data, as shown by Figure 3.2.

Customer data such as name/address is found at every node, as well as product data and site/location data. The problem that this poses, in terms of the management of redundant data, is illustrated by Figure 3.3.

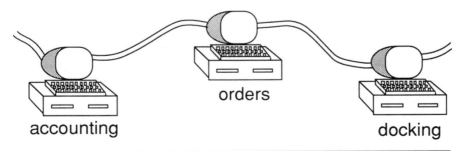

orders

accounting   docking

Figure 3.1   Three nodes in a client/server network.

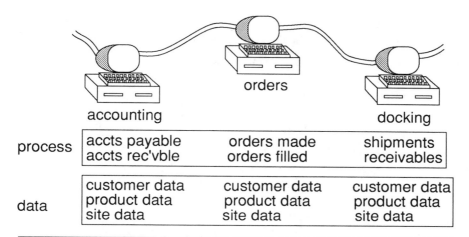

process	accts payable accts rec'vble	orders made orders filled	shipments receivables
data	customer data product data site data	customer data product data site data	customer data product data site data

Figure 3.2   Processing is different from one node to the next, but much of the data is duplicated.

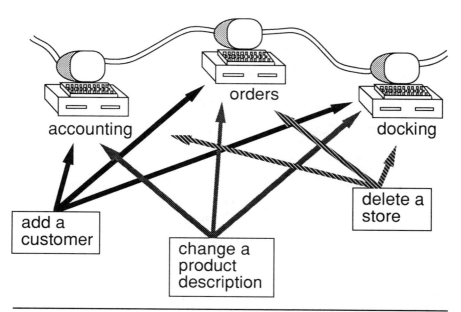

Figure 3.3   When data is redundant and needs to be changed, it must be changed in every place that it exists.

In Figure 3.3 there is a need to add a customer. To do so requires update activity at each node, as would be required in changing a product description and deleting a store from the grocer's retail system. While the activity shown in Figure 3.3 can be accomplished, given that autonomy of processing is the essence of client/server processing, it would be a short amount of time before the data is in disarray, as shown in Figure 3.4.

Figure 3.4 shows that, after a while, there are different customers throughout the network, as well as different produce and even store sites. At this point chaos reigns. Storing data centrally on a "pure" server node is one solution. But it is only a solution if data is stored *only* on the server node. The minute that clients pull the data from the server node, then start to process the data independently, and *do not* return the results of calculation back to the server node, the problem is exactly as described. When an

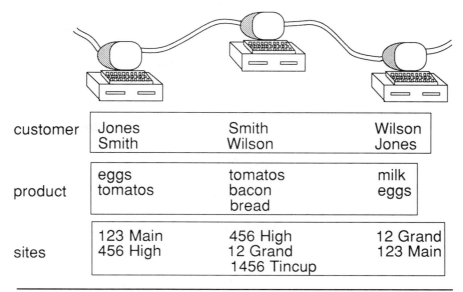

customer	Jones Smith	Smith Wilson	Wilson Jones
product	eggs tomatos	tomatos bacon bread	milk eggs
sites	123 Main 456 High	456 High 12 Grand 1456 Tincup	12 Grand 123 Main

Figure 3.4   Inconsistent data that resides at different nodes.

organization that is doing client/server processing arrives at the state depicted by Figure 3.4, it is in trouble. What happens when the accounting node requests produce information from the orders node for eggs? The accounting node recognizes eggs as a valid form of produce, but the orders node knows nothing about eggs. The data that makes the organization run is out of control in this case. A formal definition of and implementation of the system of record is needed if there is to be any control and integrity of corporate client/server processing.

How, exactly, could the system of record be implemented in a functionally oriented node resident client/server environment? The first step is to define, based on common usage of data, which node is the resident node for which data. For example, in the nodes identified in Figure 3.4, it is possible to assign "ownership" or node residency, as shown in Figure 3.5.

In Figure 3.5, the accounting node has node residency for customers; the orders node is assigned node residency for products; and the docking node is assigned residency

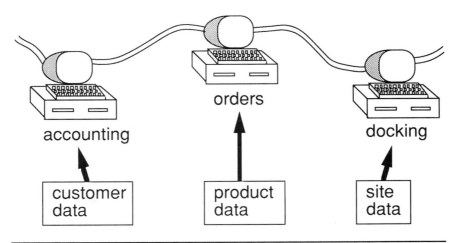

Figure 3.5   An alignment of nodes to the system of record.

for site changes. The effect of these assignments is that when changes to a customer are to be made, for example, the changes are made at the accounting node. Once the changes are made, the accounting node may (or may not) choose to notify other nodes of the changes. More importantly, if there are ever any conflicts of values, there is a single source to turn to for resolution. By definition, data in the node owning and managing the data is correct. Other nodes which are not part of the system of record are incorrect. Of course, where there is a "pure" server, and where the system of record is clearly understood and vigorously administered, the confusion in ownership and in values is resolved (or at least easily resolvable).

One of the problems with the approach shown in Figure 3.5 is that it very much favors redundancy of data. While it is simple to assign a single subject to a node (even when there is a strong affinity between the node and the data), it is likely that data will frequently be needed outside the node. For example, as is shown in Figure 3.6, suppose that data about customers is held by the accounting node. At moment n, processing at another node needs information about customer Jones; a call is made to retrieve data. Now, at moment $n+1$, the same information is needed about customer Jones. Either the data may be re-retrieved from the accounting node (thus increasing traffic across the network), or data may be stored at the using node. If data is stored at the using (i.e., client) node, it is entirely possible that the values for customer Jones may have been changed since they were originally retrieved. The tradeoff then becomes to either retrieve data fresh every time it is needed (and increase network traffic immensely), or store data, at least temporarily, at the client node and risk the possibility of operating on incorrect data.

Neither of these two options are terribly satisfactory. A third alternative—the one which most shops opt for—is

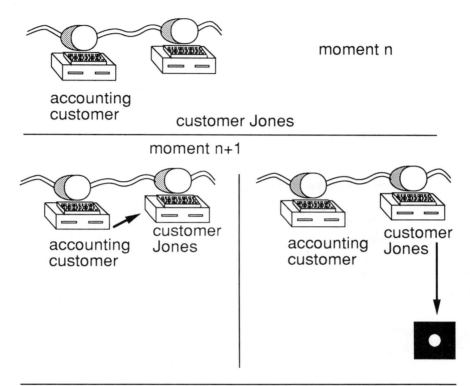

Figure 3.6   The two basic choices.

to spread data judiciously across the network or in the "pure" client, "pure" server configuration so that the node residency issue first and foremost allows data to be updated and accessed at the node and only at the node to which its system of record has been assigned. This is the optimal solution because it both minimizes the amount of network traffic and reduces the need for holding data in abeyance. In addition, the complexity of processing is grossly reduced.

What exactly might a design for the client/server environment look like in the face of the need to assign node residency judiciously? One choice is the spread of node

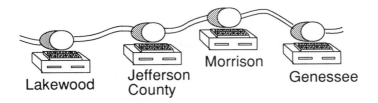

Figure 3.7   A geographic distribution of node residency.

residence based along geographic considerations. For example, suppose for a municipal police department there are different precincts in a city, as shown in Figure 3.7.

Note that data in Figure 3.8 is not redundant. Depending upon where an incident occurred, data would be placed in one or another node. Also note that Lakewood police can access Jefferson County data, but cannot change the data, because the system of record dictates that node residency be along geographical boundaries.

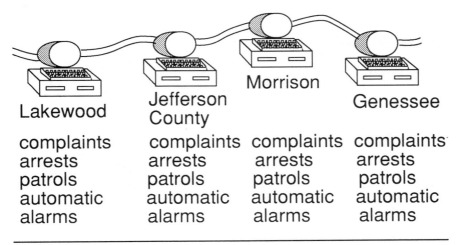

Figure 3.8   The kind of data found at each node is alike in structure and different in content.

Now suppose that the Lakewood police department does allow a case to be changed, once it is passed to another node. For example, the Morrison sheriff requests case information from Lakewood, and Lakewood agrees to allow the Morrison sheriff the right to alter the case information. This is a case of the shifting of the system of record on an individual case-by-case basis.

Should Lakewood allow the Morrison sheriff the right to change a case, the following conditions need apply:

- There is an agreed-upon time that the Morrison sheriff has to make changes. If there are no changes in the agreed-upon time, then control reverts to the Lakewood node.
- While the Morrison sheriff has the case and is considering changes, no one else may make changes to the case.
- While the Morrison sheriff has the case and is considering changes, other people may access the case as needed.
- The length of time agreed upon for study by the Morrison sheriff is stored both at the Lakewood node and the Morrison node.
- The fact that the Morrison sheriff has control of the case is public knowledge and is available to anyone.
- In any case, the system of record update control reverts back to the Lakewood node.

All of these conventions are enforced at the program level, as data is shuffled through the network. Another choice is to create a node that manages all the data, and separate nodes that process the data. Figure 3.9 describes this popular option. To summarize then, the issues of the system of record for updating operational data:

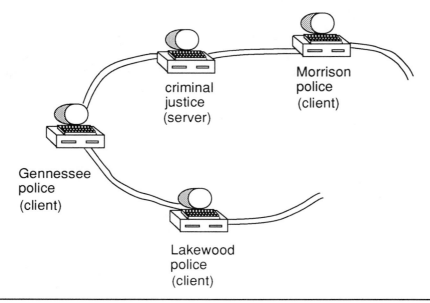

Figure 3.9   A typical configuration.

- There is a need for a clear definition of node residency if data integrity is to be maintained.
- If data integrity is not maintained, it is likely that chaos will follow.
- The primary design objective is to design node residency along lines of organizational usage.
- If an organization is oriented to different functional departments, node residency should be along departmental lines, mimicking the business responsibilities of the organization controlling the node.
- If an organization is oriented toward geographic lines of control, node residency should be split geographically.

SYSTEM OF RECORD—DSS PROCESSING

The system of record concept is equally valid for archival, time-variant data (that is, data in support of DSS processing). However, there is an essential difference between the system of record for operational data and the system of record for DSS data: Operational data is current-valued and can be updated, while archival, time-variant data, once written correctly, cannot be updated. Because archival, time-variant data cannot be updated, the nature of the system of record for client/server DSS processing is quite different from that for operational processing. The system of record for DSS processing is called the "data warehouse."

The need for the system of record for DSS processing is best illustrated in the terms of DSS processing in a client/server environment where there is no system of record. Consider the following very normal sequence of events. On day one, the accounting node captures information about customers' credit ratings, lines of business, payment histories, etc. The information is for all customers.

On day two the marketing department accesses customer data on the accounting node. The marketing department selects only customers whose credit rating is A or above.

On day two, the node responsible for management reporting seeks data about customers. Data from the accounting department about customers who have had an account since 1988 are selected.

Now marketing is asked to do an analysis on customer demographics. At the same time, management reporting is asked to do a similar analysis of customer demographics based on their data. The results of the analysis are shown in Figure 3.13.

Both marketing and management reporting started with their definition of what a customer is and produced very different results. Who is to be believed? How do you reconcile the discrepancy between the two? If you don't start with the same sets of data, how can you fault the end

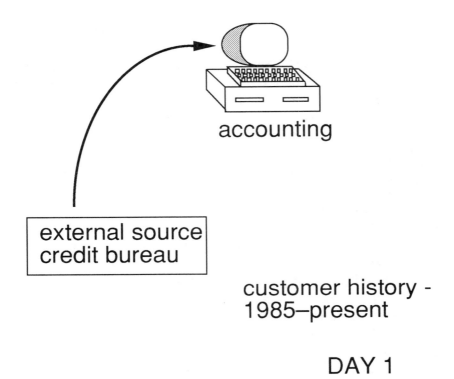

accounting

external source
credit bureau

customer history -
1985–present

DAY 1

Figure 3.10   External data entering the network.

analysis for being inconsistent? But analyzing inconsistent sets of data is only one factor contributing to inconsistency of DSS processing. Consider the client/server network for a law enforcement environment, as shown by Figure 3.14.

A report is required by the state legislature for all law enforcement agencies. Each node must prepare its report, as shown in Figure 3.15.

The results shown in Figure 3.15 are startling in that they are so different. Is one area of town that much more

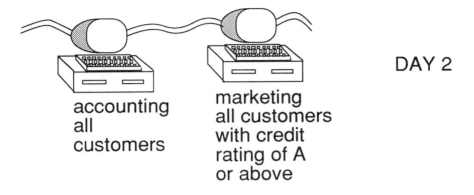

accounting
all
customers

marketing
all customers
with credit
rating of A
or above

DAY 2

Figure 3.11   Different departments have different data.

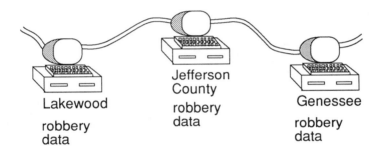

Lakewood

robbery
data

Jefferson
County
robbery
data

Genessee

robbery
data

Figure 3.12   Management reporting has yet different data
from other departments.

unsafe than the next? Is Lakewood that much more unsafe than Jefferson County or Genessee? If you judge by
the raw robbery rate, Lakewood is. But Lakewood has reported on robberies that have occurred 24 hours a day, 7
days a week. Jefferson County has reported on robberies
that have occurred Monday through Friday, 8:00 am to
5:00 pm. And Genessee has reported on robberies that
have occurred only after-hours—from 6:00 pm to 7:00 am.

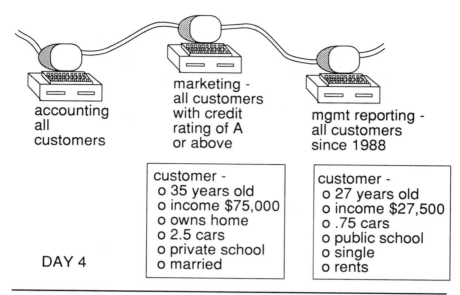

accounting
all
customers

marketing -
all customers
with credit
rating of A
or above

mgmt reporting -
all customers
since 1988

customer -
o 35 years old
o income $75,000
o owns home
o 2.5 cars
o private school
o married

customer -
o 27 years old
o income $27,500
o .75 cars
o public school
o single
o rents

DAY 4

Figure 3.13 Very different conclusions result from different base data to begin with.

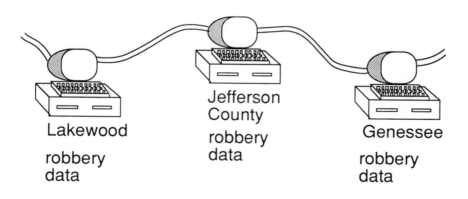

Lakewood
robbery
data

Jefferson
County
robbery
data

Genessee
robbery
data

Figure 3.14 A law enforcement network.

Jefferson
County

Lakewood

Genessee

Figure 3.15   Different data across the network.

If the time basis of data across the network used for the purposes of selecting data for analysis is not consistent, then why should unbelievable, inconsistent results surprise anyone?

But an inconsistent time basis of data is not the only reason for the unbelievability of data in the client/server environment without a system of record. A third mitigating factor is that in the client/server environment data is passed from node to node freely. Each time data is passed from one node to the next, the probability of mixing up the time basis of data or the subset of data that is being used for analysis is raised. Figure 3.16 shows the passage of data in a client/server environment.

Ultimately, the source of the data and the integrity of the data is lost. It is like the teenage parlor game where people sit around in a circle, passing a "secret" from one person to the next. When the "secret" has gone full circle, it does not even resemble what it was when it was initiated. The same effect occurs when data is passed around a client/server environment in a random, uncontrolled fashion.

External data contribute to the problem of DSS data in the client/server environment without a system of record (i.e., a data warehouse). It is very easy to enter data from a wide variety of external sources. In Figure 3.17 one node

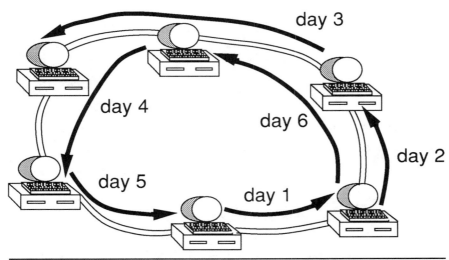

Figure 3.16   The passing of DSS data occurs randomly and frequently. Each passage of data involves the alteration of a subset of data and/or data with a different time basis.

uses Lotus 1-2-3 to enter numbers about GNP projections from the Wall Street Journal, and another node uses dbase III to enter GNP projections from Business Week.

Unfortunately, as the data is entered from each node, the source of the origin of the data is lost. The GNP projections enter the pool of data at each node and now present conflicting, unreconcilable data. External data and the loss of the source of origin, then, are additional factors why DSS processing in a client/server environment without a specifically defined system of record leads to lack of credibility.

A final reason for the lack of credibility of DSS processing in a client/server environment without a system of record is that there may be no common source of data to begin with. Suppose that state policy reporting draws upon data from the Lakewood police, and the county commis-

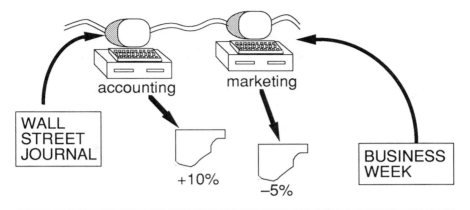

Figure 3.17   External data leading to different conclusions.

sioners draw upon data from the Jefferson County sheriff, as shown in Figure 3.18.

One report to the State says that DWI activity is up. Another report to the county avers that DWI activity is down. Since there never was a common source of data to begin with in the DSS client/server environment, why is it surprising that the analysis is so different? Without a solidly defined DSS system of record—a client/server data warehouse—the following factors contribute to chaos and unbelievability of DSS processing:

- no time basis of data,
- analysis of different subsets of data,
- "chaining" data across the network, raising the probability of the lack of credibility with each chain,
- the problem of external data, especially where external data is stripped of its source, and
- analysis done from different sources of data to begin with.

If DSS processing is to be done in a credible fashion, it must be done with the system of record—the data ware-

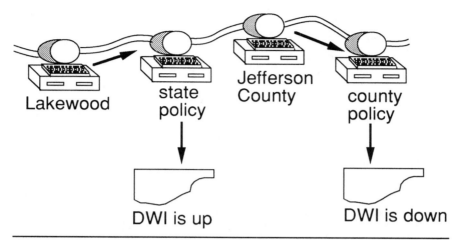

Figure 3.18 Different nodes drawing different conclusions.

house—firmly defined. In the early days of client/server processing, the phenomena described are only barely noticeable. Figure 3.19 illustrates the difference in credibility between the two environments.

Unlike the system of record for the operational environment, adopting a few conventions for programming and database design will not suffice to solve the deep seated problems of informational, analytical processing for the client/server DSS environment. We will outline some options for implementing the DSS system of record—the client/server data warehouse—in the client/server environment in the next chapter.

THE DSS SYSTEM OF RECORD/DATA WAREHOUSE

The DSS system of record—data warehouse—can be placed in several places in the client/server environment. One possibility is to place all DSS data in the system of record—data warehouse—and place the data on a separate node in the client/server network, as shown by Figure 3.20.

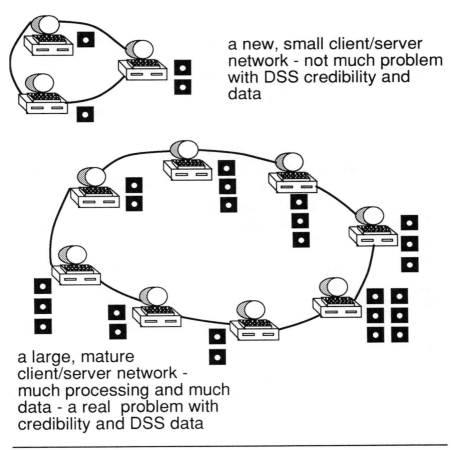

a new, small client/server network - not much problem with DSS credibility and data

a large, mature client/server network - much processing and much data - a real problem with credibility and DSS data

Figure 3.19   The size and maturity of the network makes all the difference.

The advantage with this approach is

- the processing at the DSS node is very different from the processing at other nodes, but
- the amount of data that accumulates at this node can be significant, so much so that the hardware resources that are available at the node can be stretched.

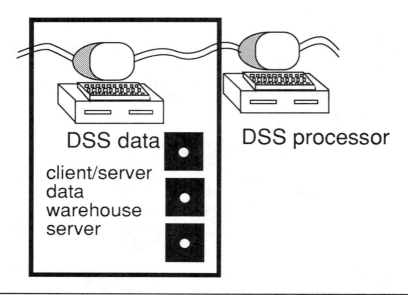

Figure 3.20   All DSS data is managed by a node in the network.

Another approach is to distribute DSS data through-out the network from node to node where each node is a server (exclusively), as shown in Figure 3.21.

The advantage of Figure 3.21 is that there is an almost infinite amount of capacity into which DSS system of record data can be expanded. The number of nodes over which the system of record-data warehouse-data can be expanded is unending. The problems with this approach to distributing DSS system of record data are that

• the data is physically removed to different nodes. This means that blanket access to data that happens to pre-side on more than one node, a practice that is normal in the world of DSS processing, requires many re-sources to accomplish.

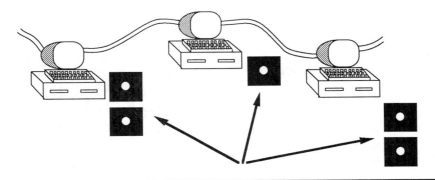

Figure 3.21   Some DSS data at each node.

- because the data is physically located at different nodes, it is a temptation to independently alter—add, delete, modify—data at each node. The result is a lack of integration and uniformity, which defeats one of the main purposes of even having a client/server data warehouse in the first place.

Another option is to spread the client/server system of record over multiple nodes (as previously shown) except to allow both data warehouse data and DSS processing to exist on the node simultaneously. Figure 3.22 shows this option.

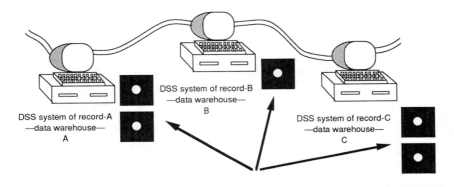

Figure 3.22   Some DSS data at each node.

The problem with this option is that it mixes data warehouse data management and processing with analytical DSS processing on the same node. As long as there is little data, little access to the data warehouse data, and limited DSS processing, this option will work. But when any one of the three conditions change, the option proves to be less than satisfactory. If there is much data to be managed, then the data warehouse data should be placed on a separate server exclusive node. If there is much access to the data warehouse data, then the data warehouse data should be placed on a separate server exclusive node. Or if there is much DSS processing that is occurring, then the data warehouse data should be placed on a separate server exclusive node. In the final analysis, trying to use a node for general purposes for DSS processing—doing both processing and data warehouse management—is not a good idea.

A third approach is to store DSS system of record data off in a different environment, but one that is available by means of a network. Figure 3.23 shows this possibility.

The approach shown in Figure 3.23 solves both problems associated with locating the DSS system of record data at a node or distributing the data across different nodes. One implication of this scenario is that DSS processing is the only type of processing done using data warehouse data.

The choice described—using a mainframe for the client/server data warehouse—is an excellent way to segue between the mainframe environment and the client/server environment. Figure 3.24 shows this popular scenario.

Figure 3.24 shows that the data warehouse is built from data gleaned from the operational/legacy systems environment. The data warehouse then becomes a massive server, serving the client/server environment. There is a word of caution here, however. In this scenario *only* DSS process-

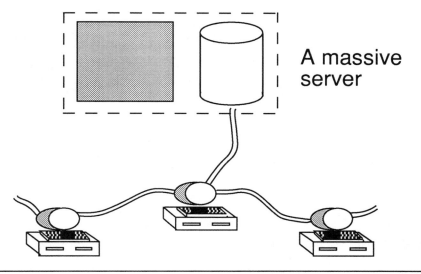

Figure 3.23   Mainframe/mini DSS data server. Another alternative.

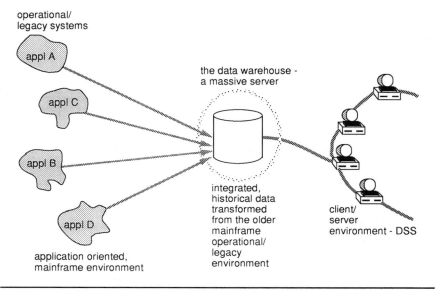

Figure 3.24   Using the data warehouse to segue between mainframe legacy systems and the client/server environment.

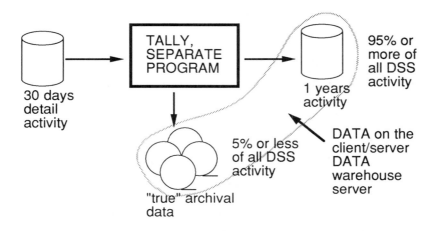

Figure 3.25   Different levels of granularity in the client/server data warehouse.

ing is being done at the client/server environment. Despite this restriction, the scenario shows that a good first step of going to the client/server environment is that of creating the data warehouse from operation/legacy systems.

One characteristic of DSS system of record—data warehouse—data is that much storage space is consumed. Even in a modest sized environment, it is normal for the volume of data to grow to large proportions. For this reason, it is common practice to introduce the concept of different levels of granularity—different levels of detail—for DSS data in the client/server data warehouse. An example best illustrates the issues of granularity. Suppose a real estate company keeps track of leads, sales, calls, etc. for 30 days as a regular part of operational processing. Now, suppose there is a desire to keep up to one year's data on sales calls for DSS processing and analysis, as shown by Figure 3.25.

It does not take a deep analysis to see that much DSS data will aggregate shortly in the DSS data warehouse if each detail fed to it is stored in the DSS system of record.

A decision is made to tally detailed records into a higher level of granularity as the data ages. For example, one file in the client/server data warehouse is sales calls by agent by month. Each month each agent has his/her total number of sales calls recorded. Another file in the client/server data warehouse is number of viewers by property by month. For each property being managed, each month the number of viewers is tallied. Sales by month are tallied as well. The effect of tallying basic detailed data into monthly files is the creation of condensed data. The condensed monthly files are very efficient to store and to access on the server.

However, if it is necessary to dig into the historical detail, a true archival file is kept as well on the server. Detailed data is simply "dumped" into the true archival file. If the condensed file is properly designed the vast majority of DSS processing is able to be done on the less granular, more condensed data.

Granularity of data is the first consideration of building the DSS system of record—client/server data warehouse. The second consideration in the building of the DSS system of record is that of integration of data. In order to be effective, data in the DSS system of record—client/server data warehouse—must be integrated across multiple applications. It is normal for client/server operational processing to have an application orientation. But as data passes from the operational applications to the DSS environment, data takes on an integrated orientation. If operational data is allowed to pass to the DSS system of record—the data warehouse—and retain the application orientation, much of the usefulness of the DSS system of record environment is lost. The integration of data as it passes to the client/server data warehouse normally entails conversion, logic, condensation, summarization, and filtering.

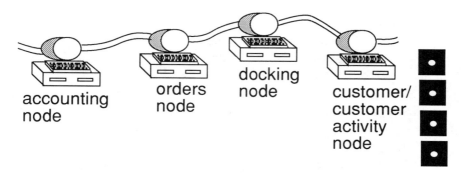

Figure 3.26   Different operational nodes passing data to the system of record.

For example, as shown in Figure 3.26, suppose that three operational nodes—an accounting node, an orders processing node, and a docking node—all pass data to the customer/customer activity DSS system of record. Even though the different nodes pass different data to the DSS system of record, in order to be effective the data must be integrated. This means, for example, that a customer known to accounting is the same customer that is known to docking. Or, for example, when orders processing reports a date in a format YY/MM/DD, the date is recognized and consistent with that in docking. Or, for example, when orders processing describes part ABC as a "screw," the ABC in docking processing is also known as a "screw." In short, when data arrives at the DSS system of record—the client/server data warehouse—it is known consistently across the DSS environment as the same thing.

Another important characteristic of the transformation of operational data to data in the DSS system of record—client/server data warehouse—is that DSS system of record data is "time-variant." Time-variant data in the data warehouse implies that the key structure of the data is appended with some date:

- key + from date + to date
- key + effective date
- key + as of date

Data coming from the operational environment seldom has a date orientation. A major part of the transformation of operational to DSS data, then, is that of key transformation.

In many cases, the data going into the client/server data warehouse can be considered to be "snapshot" data. An event occurs in the operational environment that causes a snapshot of operational data to be taken. The snapshot, along with the time and date the snapshot was taken, is then stored in the client/server data warehouse.

Another common client/server data warehouse structure is that of summary data. Not only is detail stored in the client/server environment, but summary data is stored as well. The date of the summarization is usually stored along with the summary as well.

Of course periodically, data must be removed from the data warehouse. In some cases, this means that data is discarded upon removal. In other cases the data is merely moved to another storage media (i.e., "deep freeze") archival storage.

Almost universally, the criteria for moving data out of the data warehouse is based on age. The older the data gets, the less likely it is to be used in the data warehouse.

SUMMARY

In this chapter we have explored the system of record in both the operational and the DSS environment. In the operational environment the system of record is defined by node residency, where control of update resides at each node. Node residency is defined by a functional alignment with the organization. If the organization is divided along the lines of different departments doing different functions, such as accounting, marketing, etc., then node residency is likewise defined. If the organization has a geographic split where different geographic units are involved, then node residency is done along the lines of geographic splits.

The system of record in the DSS environment—the client/server data warehouse has an essentially different implementation from the system of record for operational processing because DSS data, once correctly recorded, is not updated. The factors that contribute to a need for a system of record for DSS data are

- analytical processing across different sets of data,
- no time basis of DSS data,
- multiple levels of extraction, each of which exaggerate the probabilities of data disintegrity,
- external data, especially external data whose source has been stripped away, and
- no common source of data to begin with.

The characteristics of the client/server data warehouse are

- subject orientation,
- integration,
- non volatility once the snapshot is made,
- time variancy.

4

Configurations

Our plans miscarry because they have no aim. When a man does not know what harbor he is making for, no wind is the right wind.

Seneca

To fulfill the need for a separation of operational and DSS data and processing, there are multiple implementation options for the client/server environment. Figure 4.1 shows the general options.

The options are

- operational only processing in the client/server environment,
- DSS only processing in the client/server environment,
- a central DSS system of record store—the client/server data warehouse—coupled with networked operational and DSS nodes, and
- one or more exclusive server DSS nodes coupled with networked operational nodes and DSS processor nodes,

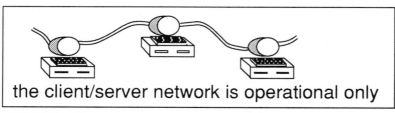

the client/server network is operational only

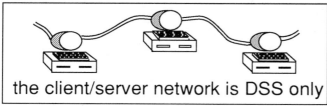

the client/server network is DSS only

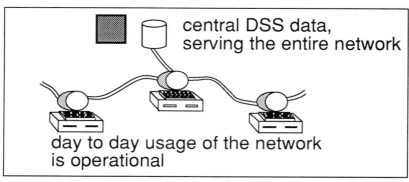

central DSS data,
serving the entire network

day to day usage of the network
is operational

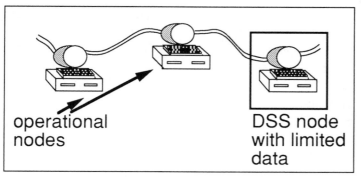

operational
nodes

DSS node
with limited
data

Figure 4.1   Some common configurations of DSS data and
operational data and processing in the client/
server environment.

• Linked rings where a ring is either totally DSS or is totally operational.

The option of distributing DSS data from node to node is not viable for the reasons previously mentioned.

A CRITIQUE

Operational only client/server processing. One of the most common options, it is perhaps the simplest. There is no need for time variant data in this node.

DSS only processing. This option does not commonly occur. However, when it does occur, it is a fairly attractive option because there is no mixing of operational and DSS data and processing. In this case the operational system of record may be spread over more than one node, or there may be an operational server that manages data exclusively for operational only processors.

Central DSS system of record coupled with networked operational and DSS nodes. This most convenient option has many advantages. Operational processing is placed conveniently on nodes while the larger store of DSS data is placed on a larger server. DSS processing is done on separate nodes. The DSS environment can placed on one rings(s) and operational processing can be placed on another ring(s).

One or more DSS processing nodes are mixed with operational nodes. This option applies only to the case where there is limited DSS data and processing. In many ways this option is a transition option that is valid only as long as there is a modicum of DSS data.

AN EXAMPLE

The best way to explain these options is in terms of an example. Suppose a western states realty company is headquartered in Denver. The realty company has branch offices in every major city in the western part of the United States. A series of wide area networks are constructed, as shown in Figure 4.2.

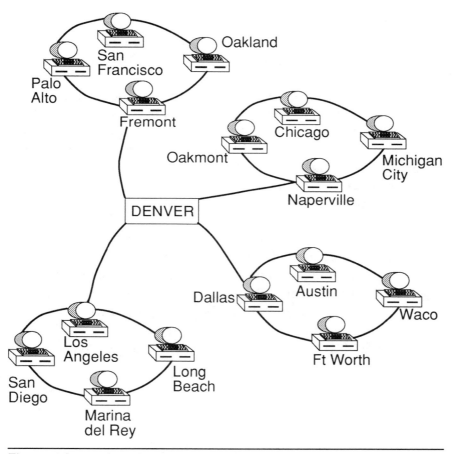

Figure 4.2   A real estate network incorporating several local client/server networks.

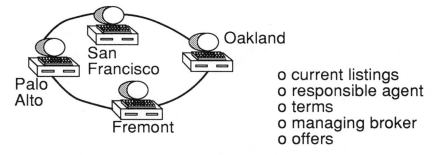

Figure 4.3   Client server processing for Bay Area real estate.

Most western and midwest cities are part of the networks shown in Figure 4.2. At the center is the real estate management in Denver. The first technological configuration to be discussed is that of the operational only client/server network. Figure 4.3 shows the client/server environment for the San Francisco Bay area.

In Figure 4.3, the data held at each node is for

- current listings,
- the agent responsible for booking/selling the listing,
- the terms for each property for sale,
- who the managing broker is, and
- what offers have been made on the property.

Any piece of real estate in the Bay Area that is under the auspices of the company is in the network. If a property is on Market Street, it is contained in the San Francisco node. If a property is in Berkeley, it is in the Oakland node. If the property is in Gilroy, it is found in the San Jose node, and so forth.

The network contains only those properties for sale. Once the sale is made, the property is deleted from the system. This configuration is an example of an operational only client/server environment.

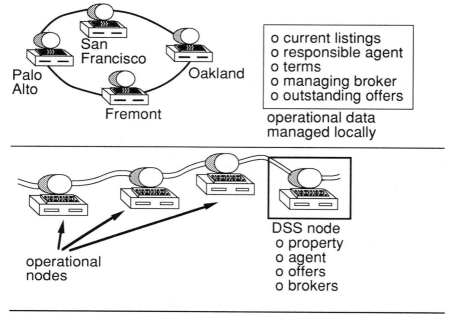

Figure 4.4   Mixing node types.

The second configuration is that of a DSS only client/ server environment. This configuration is somewhat of an anomaly—it infrequently exists. In the example of the Denver-based real estate company, suppose, at the Denver hub, there existed a client/server environment such as that depicted by Figure 4.4.

In Figure 4.4, some of the nodes represent the DSS component of the home office—accounting, marketing, sales, etc. Another node(s) hosts the DSS system of record, containing integrated historical data for properties, agents, listing, etc.

Our third option, a popular configuration, is the client/ server operational network and the central, large DSS repository of DSS system of record—client/server data warehouse—data. Figure 4.5 shows a possible configuration.

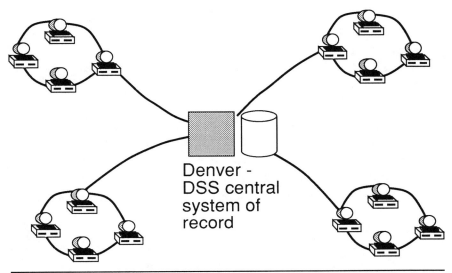

Denver -
DSS central
system of
record

Figure 4.5   A central system of record.

In Denver there is a central repository of DSS data—the data warehouse. This data reflects the integrated corporate perspective over a long period of time. From this central repository of corporate DSS data reports are run, such as

- month by month listings for the past 2 years,
- number of active agents by office by month for the last year, and
- a comparison of the length of time a house has been on the market in San Francisco for the past 6 months versus homes in Chicago, and so forth.

In short, a view of data over time, looking across the corporation in an integrated manner is afforded by the DSS system of record—the client/server data warehouse. At the local level there are multiple client/server networks that serve the day-to-day operational needs of the local office. Periodically, depending on the data, information is passed from the local, client/server level to the central, DSS data warehouse server.

A final possibility (although one that is fraught with pitfalls) is that shown by Figure 4.6.

Figure 4.6 shows that each local client/server network has one or more nodes dedicated to DSS processing. The DSS system of record is distributed to the different nodes in this case. As long as the DSS analysis that is occurring is local and limited, there is no problem associated with Figure 4.6. However, the configuration shown does not

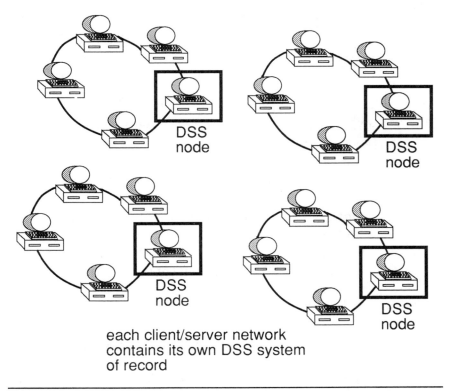

each client/server network
contains its own DSS system
of record

Figure 4.6   Each client/server network contains its own DSS system of record.

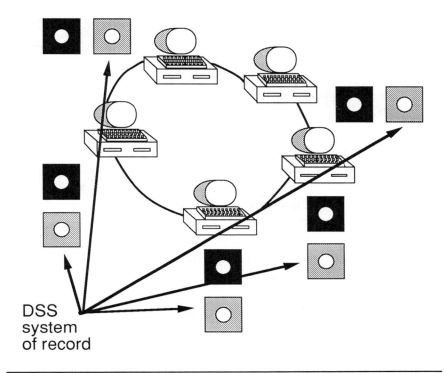

DSS
system
of record

Figure 4.7   Distributing the system of record across different
nodes. There is no corporate view in this case.

support corporate-wide DSS processing. The ability to
look at DSS processing on a corporate basis is greatly impaired by the configuration shown for Figure 4.7.

THE "PURE" SERVER ENVIRONMENT AND THE
DATA WAREHOUSE

The "pure" server environment—where a server is dedicated solely and exclusively to the management of data
and the servicing of clients—is a natural fit for the system
of record—the data warehouse—in the client/server envi-

ronment. However, there are some special considerations the designer should be aware of in making this selection. The first consideration is that of volume of data needed.

It is a temptation to say that the needed DASD capacity is slightly more than the total data that will exist on the server. In other words, if there are to be 1 gigabytes of data on the data warehouse, then the server needs 1.5 gigabytes' capacity. Such is not the case at all. As a rule you need to have 4 to 6 times the storage capacity on the server times the amount of data that will be in the data warehouse. There are several reasons for this:

- Data always requires a "fit" factor.
- Indexing space needs to be calculated in as well.
- Spooling space is needed.
- Formatting space is needed.
- System workspace—for joins, etc.—is needed.
- Sort space is needed.
- Other system miscellaneous space is needed.

There is then a need for much more raw storage capacity than will be needed for the data warehouse.

Because so much will be needed, it is a temptation (and a real possibility) to divide the data warehouse data over more than one "pure" server. Figure 4.8 shows this option.

Figure 4.8 shows that the data warehouse resides over more than one server. This configuration works well as long as queries are restricted to one processor or the other. But when a query does extensive access of data over multiple servers, there is a basic problem, as shown in Figure 4.9.

In Figure 4.9, there is no problem on the left. But in the case shown on the right, where extensive data is accessed from more than one server, there quickly appears problems in

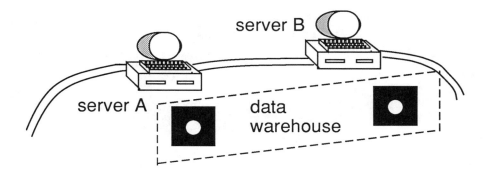

Figure 4.8   The data warehouse spread over the two
servers.

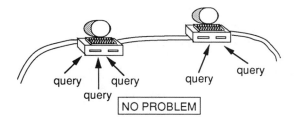

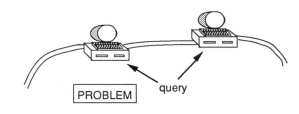

Figure 4.9   What happens when a query operates against a
single node or more than one node in the
distributed data warehouse environment.

- network traffic,
- overflow of system work areas, and
- inability to handle joins elegantly (or at all), and so forth.

If data is to be divided over more than one server, very careful attention must be paid to exactly how the split in data is to be made.

SUMMARY

There are many possible configurations for the management of operational and DSS processing in the client/server environment.

Some of the more popular configurations are

- no DSS processing, operational only,
- no operational processing, DSS only,
- centralized DSS processing, distributed operational processing, and
- decentralized DSS processing, distributed operational processing.

There are, of course, other configurations that are basically subsets of these. Each configuration has its advantages and disadvantages.

5

Performance in the Client/Server Environment

Nothing is more terrible than activity without insight.

Thomas Carlyle

Performance in the computer environment has been an issue from the first Fortran program on all the way to today's C++ programs. Performance is a burning issue in some environments, such as the online, transaction mode of operation. And performance is likewise an issue in the client/server environment, although it takes on a different form and a different demeanor from performance as it is known as in those other environments.

Why is performance an issue at all in the client/server environment? It is a temptation to say that if in the client/server environment performance ever becomes a problem, a larger processor can be installed at any given node. A faster pc or a workstation with more memory can be bought, thus improving performance. In doing so, performance can be boosted. Or, in a worst scenario, the processing done at any node can be divided over more than one node. In some cases such a division can be made and a boost in performance is the result. But addressing performance solely at the hardware level is as much a mistake in the client/server environment as it is in any other environment. For instance, there is a limit to the size of machine that you would ever want to buy to serve as a node in a client/server environment. In addition, there are many occasions where splitting the workload over more than one node will not boost performance. In some cases the workload is not easily divided. In other cases, the workload can be divided, but because of single threading of data, there is no performance gain.

Performance is an issue, then, because when a client/server environment fails to perform:

- the user's time is wasted,
- more expense may accrue because of hardware expenditure, and
- the solution to easing the performance problem often is not as simple as merely buying a larger processor or upgrading a network.

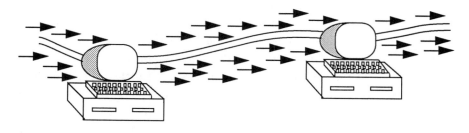

Figure 5.1   The client/server network is flooded with many messages.

PERFORMANCE PROBLEM MANIFESTATION

There are several ways performance problems rise to the surface in the client/server environment.

- Network flooding due to many small messages being sent.

Even though this phenomenon can occur, it is usually the least likely cause of performance problems in the client/server environment.

- Network flooding due to many large messages being sent. This phenomenon can occur as a regular matter of course. It is much more common than the preceding phenomenon.

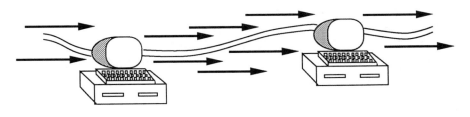

Figure 5.2   The client/server network is flooded with many long messages.

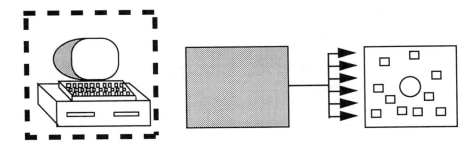

Figure 5.3   Massive access of data, locking up the node during the retrieval process. The node is so busy it cannot service new requests. New requests have to be queued.

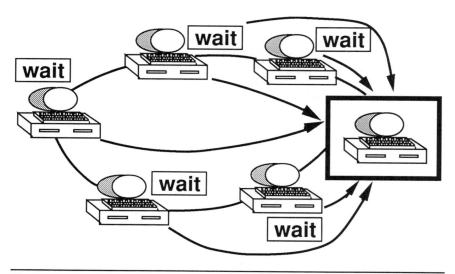

Figure 5.4   This node has become a hot spot.

- Node "lockup" due to massive access of data. This phenomenon is easily the most common reason for poor performance.

When node lockup occurs, the effect on the network usually becomes noticeable, and that effect is the "network hotspot" phenomena. A node becomes a "hot spot" in a network when the node essentially fills up with work and is unable to process any new requests for data sent to it. In essence, the "hot spot" becomes the "weak link" in the network. Figure 5.4 illustrates a node that is overly busy and has become a hot spot.

- Node lockup due to data locking. In the case where data can be passed to another node for update, the data becomes "locked" until either the time reserved for the data is passed, or until the data is returned in an updated state, as shown by Figure 5.5. Locking is espe-

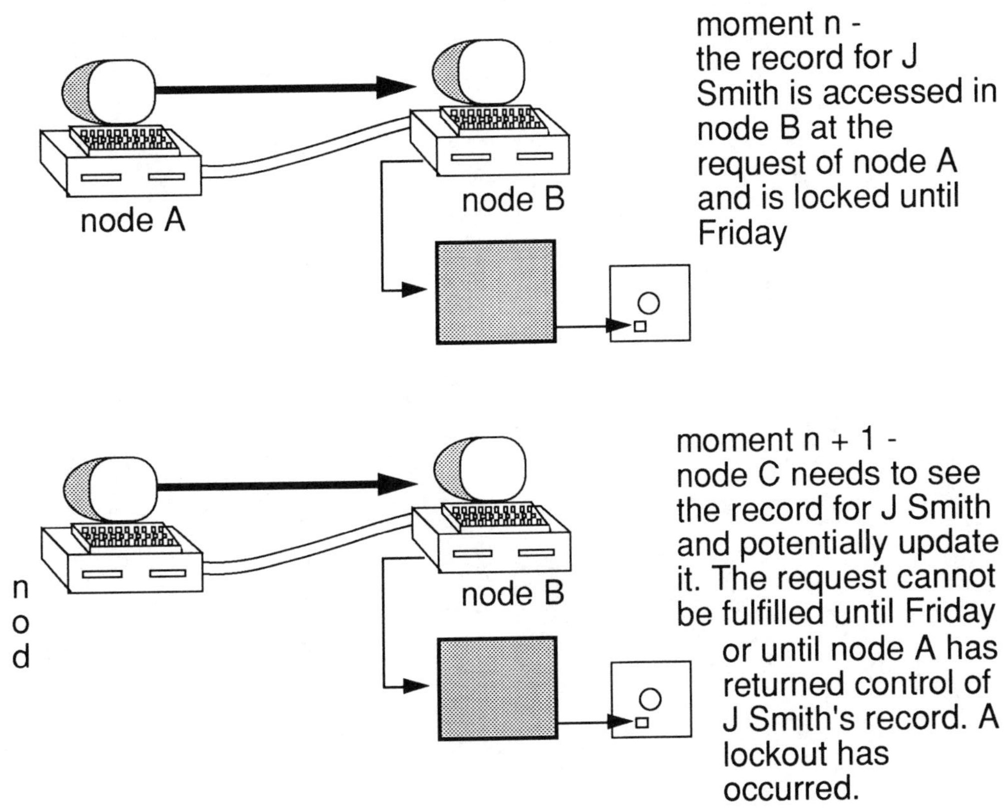

moment n -
the record for J
Smith is accessed in
node B at the
request of node A
and is locked until
Friday

node A

node B

moment n + 1 -
node C needs to see
the record for J Smith
and potentially update
it. The request cannot
be fulfilled until Friday
or until node A has
returned control of
J Smith's record. A
lockout has
occurred.

node B

n
o
d

Figure 5.5   Locking and performance.

cially an issue where a careful job of defining and executing the system of record is implemented.

In Figure 5.5 a node has requested access and update capability to J. Smith's record. Access is granted and control is passed until Friday. Later in the day another request from another node is passed for J. Smith's data. Only now, the request cannot be honored because control no longer lies with the resident node. Completion of the request cannot be completed until Friday, or until the data is returned from the original node to whom control was passed. Performance turns really sour for the node waiting in abeyance. There probably are other ways in which performance may become an issue in the client/server environment, but these reasons are the most common.

In an attempt to position the organization in as proactive a state as possible, what, from a design perspective, can be done to circumvent these problems of performance? The following are some suggestions that should be applied at the moment of design.

Program design. When a program makes a request for data outside the resident node, the request should always be for limited amounts of data. Requesting access to very large amounts of data should be done only if absolutely necessary.

When a request for data outside the resident node is made, the request should be for access only to the data. Only in the case where update is made should the request for data be made in the update mode.

When a request for data is made outside the resident node, the length of time the data is to be locked should be minimal.

When a requesting program or a server program runs for a truly long time, it is a good practice to break the program into more, shorter programs. Not only does this enhance performance, but it can save considerable rerun time. Check points should be periodically taken.

When a program makes a request for data from a server, only data that is needed should be requested. If the requesting node already has some of the data in hand, there is no sense in requesting all over again.

When a program makes a request for data from a server, the data should be completely delivered to the requesting node before indexing is done.

When a program makes a request for data from a server, the sequence of the data as it is stored and the sequence of the data as it will be delivered, needs to be taken into consideration.

When a program accesses data, the data should be indexed. Blanket searches of a database where there is no index are not recommended.

When a program accesses more than one record, data access and storage should be buffered.

Node residency. Node residency should be designed on a probability of access/update basis. The data resident at a node should have the highest probability of access/update at that node. In other words, if data is going to be frequently accessed/updated at one particular node, then the data belongs in the node residency definition.

Data design. Data should be grouped into two categories: data that is frequently accessed and data that is frequently updated. For data that is frequently accessed but not frequently updated, the internal design should be physically denormalized. For data that is frequently updated but not frequently accessed, data should be physically normalized in a non redundant manner. The whole issue of normalization/denormalization of data harks back to subject of I/Os. What is an I/O? An I/O stands for "input/output" operation—in other words, a physical read or write of data. Figure 5.6 illustrates an I/O.

Why is an I/O a relevant subject to performance in the client/server environment? I/O's are relevant because they are performed at substantially lower speeds than internal operations of the computer. Every time the computer has to slow down to do an I/O, performance is impaired. This slowdown is especially harmful where the operating system runs in a single-thread state, which is very typical of the workstations and pc's found in the client/server environment. The strategy then to achieve high levels of performance in the client/server environment is to do as few I/O's as possible. However, achieving the strategy of I/O minimization is not a straightforward task. The amount of I/O used by an application in the client/server environment is directly a function of the database design on which the application runs.

Consider two client/server programs, A and B, which perform exactly the same function, as shown in Figure

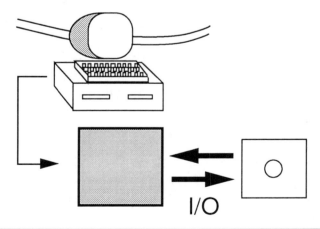

Figure 5.6   I/O occurs as data passes either to or from storage to the executing program.

5.7. Programs A and B are identical, with one exception. The data that program A runs on is widely scattered across disk storage. The data that program B runs on is aggregated into a few physical locations on desk storage. Program B runs much more quickly than Program A simply because program B does much less I/O than program A. Yet both programs accomplish the same function.

The temptation then, is to rush in and say that the database design for program B is a superior design (and in fact, it may very well be). However, it is entirely possible that the design that makes program B run so efficiently for one program makes every other program that accesses the data run inefficiently. The optimal design is not a function in which one or two programs are optimized for performance; the optimal design is a function of the total workload that must be satisfied.

A general approach to organizing data for database design is the practice of normalization of data. (Note: This has been true for systems long before there was a client/server environment.) Much has been written on the subject of normalization and the techniques for achieving normalized design. In short, the practice of normalization of data organizes data around a "natural" occurrence of data elements. A natural occurrence of data is one where attributes of data are grouped together into a table where all attributes depend on the key of the grouping of data for their existence. Some simple examples of normalization are

person	part	order
SSNO	part number (key)	date of order
age	qty on hand	order amount
height	description	order status
weight	unit of measure	item ordered
DOB		who ordered by
sex		

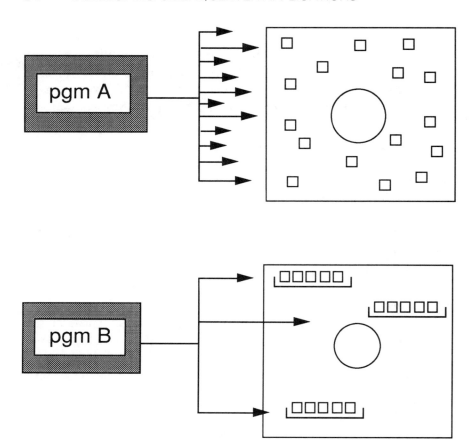

Figure 5.7   Program A and program B do the same thing,
but the data that is accessed by program B is
physically arranged in a compact, tightly
organized manner. Program B operates in a
much more efficient fashion than program A.

In the cases shown, the attributes of the data depend directly on the key for their existence.

Normalization of data is a natural, good way to form the basis of database design. However, one result of the normalization process is that of producing many tables (or groups of attributes), each of which only has a few attributes, as shown by Figure 5.8. If the tables shown in Figure 5.8 are literally turned into physical database design, then the effect will be the use of much I/O, as described earlier.

A more sophisticated approach is to use the normalized tables as a basis for "logical" database design. Then, based upon the processing needs of the entire environment, physically denormalize data.

The normalized tables are physically reorganized to accommodate the processing that is to be done.

One common way to achieve physical optimization of the placement of data is to merge tables together. Merging the many, small normalized tables together has the effect of reducing the amount of work needed to be done by the system. The fewer, longer tables require less I/O for manipulation, as seen in Figure 5.9.

Now that the data is physically merged together, it is efficient to access. It should be noted that physical denormalization of data doesn't necessarily imply negat-

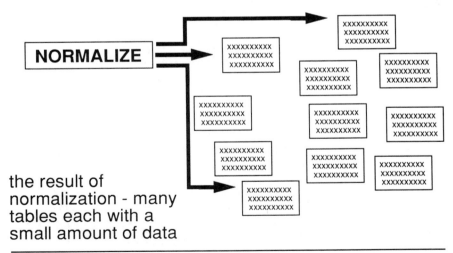

the result of normalization - many tables each with a small amount of data

Figure 5.8   The result of normalization—many tables each with a small amount of data.

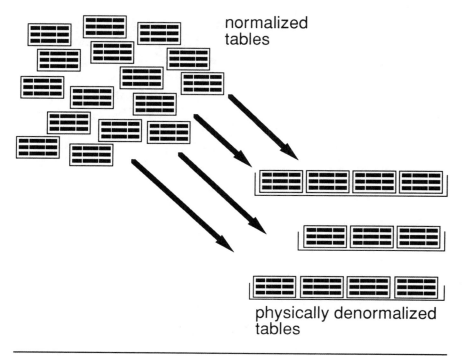

normalized
tables

physically denormalized
tables

Figure 5.9   Condensing data for performance.

ing the reasons for normalization in the first place. There are several common design techniques for the physical denormalization of data:

- selective introduction of redundant data, in order to avoid unnecessary I/O at the moment of access,
- merging of tables together, based on common keys and a common access of data together,
- creating arrays of data in a row, and
- further separation of data into smaller tables, when the probability of access of data is very different.
- introduction of derived or calculated data when that data is frequently accessed and calculated once.

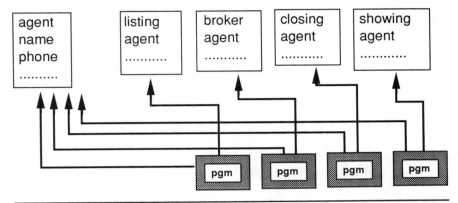

Figure 5.10   Each time listing data, broker data, closing data, and showing data are accessed, the agent's name and phone number needs to be accessed as well. However, the agent's name and phone number exist in a single table in another place. The result is much processing in order to access popular data that is physically normalized.

How is it that selective creation of redundant data can help performance in the case of data that is infrequently updated? Consider the design of a real estate system. Suppose that data is normalized, as shown in Figure 5.10.

In Figure 5.10 the name and phone number exist in a single place. References to the agent exist in systems that process listings, brokerages, closings, and open houses. Because data is normalized and non redundant, the agent's name and phone do not appear in any data other than that directly relating to the agent. The net result is that programs that process listing and brokerage information, and the like, must go to the single source where name and phone number is, which incurs much I/O. An alternative design is to include an agent's name and phone number where used with other information, as

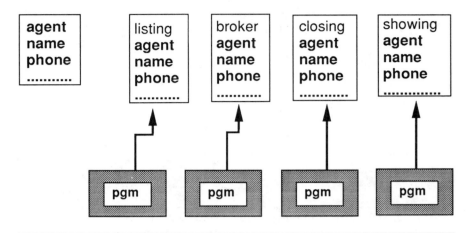

Figure 5.11   Agent name and phone number have been
placed with data with whom they are regularly
accessed. The result is that the many programs
that need to see agent name and phone number
are very efficient in their operation.

shown in Figure 5.11. As long as the name and phone
number are stable, there is very little penalty in organizing data this way. The programs that process listing information, for example, do not need to use an I/O to find
out what the responsible agent's name and phone number
is. Selectively creating redundant data is not the only
form of physical denormalization that can be useful. Figure 5.12 shows three tables that relate to a broker.

   In order to access broker information from each table,
multiple I/O's must be done. An alternative design is to
merge the tables together, as shown. Once the tables are
merged together, their access is efficient—only one I/O is
required where previously three I/O's were required. The
effectiveness of this design technique of merging tables
together depends on several factors:

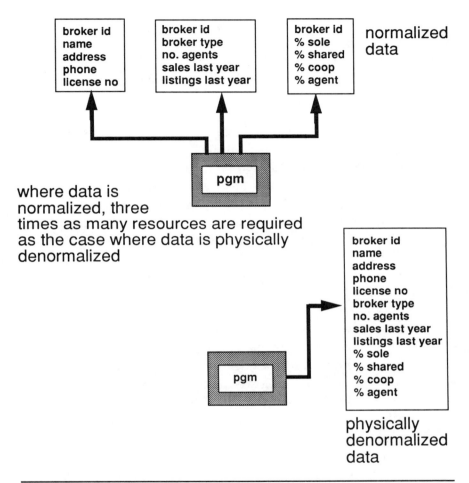

Figure 5.12   An example of merging tables to improve performance.

- Are the tables that are being merged accessed together?
- Do the tables that are being merged have a common key?
- Does it make sense logically to merge the tables?

A third design technique that is useful in creating high performance is that of creating arrays of data within a row. Figure 5.13 shows that there are four separate records for the showing of a home. Each time a program wants to look at all the records, four I/O's are consumed (one for each record). An alternative design is to create a single record with four slots for data. In this case, only one I/O is required.

The technique of creating arrays of data must be used carefully, since it is not applicable in every case. Some of the criteria that apply to its usage are:

- when the number of occurrences are predictable,
- when the occurrences are inserted sequentially,
- when there is not much data associated with each occurrence,
- when the occurrences are accessed together, and so forth.

The next standard technique for physical denormalization of data calls for data to be split into even smaller tables when there is a large discrepancy in the probability of access of data. Figure 5.14 shows an example of this type of physical denormalization.

In Figure 5.14, the attributes of a bank account—balance, domicile, and date opened—are grouped together. However, bank balance is a very popular attribute and is frequently accessed, whereas domicile and date opened are not used frequently at all. It therefore makes sense to split these attributes of data into their own separate tables. Balance information can be moved to storage that is readily accessible, while domicile and date opened may be moved off, even to floppy disk.

In the case where data is going to be updated frequently, the data should probably be left in the normalized state. There are two reasons for this.

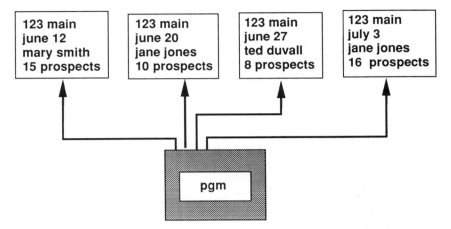

accessing normalized data where each row is a separate physical record. Much I/O is required.

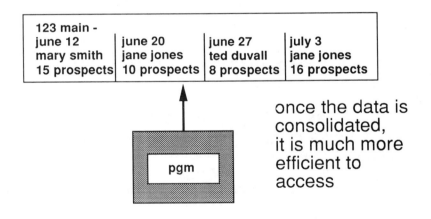

once the data is consolidated, it is much more efficient to access

Figure 5.13   Once the data is consolidated, it is much more efficient to access.

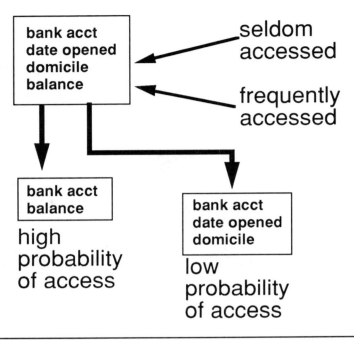

Figure 5.14   Different probabilities of access.

1. Normalized data is nonredundant. Therefore when up-date occurs, the update affects only a minimal amount of data.
2. Normalized data breaks data into small units. As data is being updated, the unit of data is locked. Therefore the locking of small units of data ensures that only the minimal amount of data is locked. The process of de-sign, in its entirety, is depicted by Figure 5.15.

Another useful design practice is to precalculate data that is known to be frequently accessed. For example, if it is known that daily sales are to be calculated and accessed many times, it makes sense to calculate it once and place the data where it can be commonly accessed. The practice

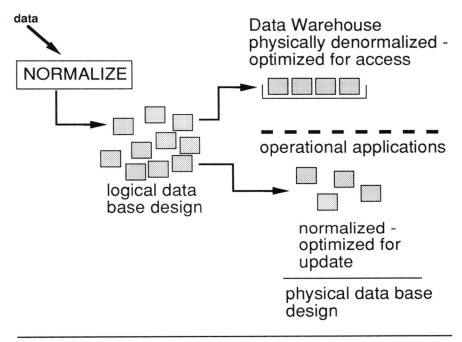

Figure 5.15   Database design steps.

of creating derived data makes sense when data is used frequently and calculated once.

OTHER PERFORMANCE PRACTICES

The preceding discussions describe the design practices for performance that need to be adopted for the client/server environment. Indeed, for the organization that wishes to take a proactive stance toward performance, these practices and guidelines are strongly recommended. However, performance doesn't end here. Another mandatory practice in the client/server environment is that of periodically reorganizing data on hard disk. The data that is on hard disk usually quickly becomes "fractured." When data becomes fractured, it resides on different blocks or sectors of hard disk. What happens when a record resides on more than one block of data is that multiple I/O's are needed to make a single access of data. For this reason, periodically hard disks should be reorganized.

In addition, occasionally data needs to be purged. Purging is usually done on a date-activated basis.

SUMMARY

The design practices that will greatly enhance performance in the client/server environment are:

- proper selection of node residency,
- adding resources as needed,
- creating many small requests for data, rather than fewer large requests for data,
- avoiding massive node access of data, or breaking massive accesses into a series of smaller accesses,
- normalizing data that is predominantly updated,
- normalizing, then denormalizing, data that is predominantly accessed.

6

Metadata and the Client/Server Environment

Drive thy business; let it not drive thee.

Benjamin Franklin (1706–1790)

Metadata is data about data. Metadata typically describes, either actively or by default, such things as structure of data, attributes, physical characteristics of attributes, keys, measurement of attributes, and so forth. Metadata describes the content of data and structure of data that allow programs to communicate with and access data, as shown by Figure 6.1.

A simple example of one form of metadata is shown in Figure 6.2.

Figure 6.2 shows the description of the layout of data in a COBOL-like format. The file layout is for parts in a warehouse and shows such fields as part number, description, quantity on hand, etc. The grouping, structure and physical characteristics of the data are shown as well. The dy-

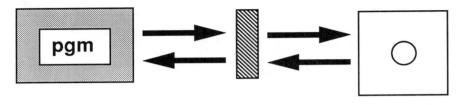

Figure 6.1   Metadata—filtering, translating request from program to data, and vice versa.

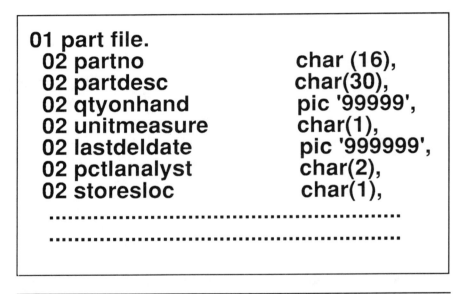

```
01 part file.
   02 partno              char (16),
   02 partdesc            char(30),
   02 qtyonhand           pic '99999',
   02 unitmeasure         char(1),
   02 lastdeldate         pic '999999',
   02 pctlanalyst         char(2),
   02 storesloc           char(1),
   .........................................
   .........................................
```

Figure 6.2   A simple example of metadata.

namics of how metadata is used during the execution of a program is illustrated by Figure 6.3.

A request is made to access data through a READ statement issued by the programmer. The location of the data is determined, usually by accessing an index. After the index is located and the raw data is found, the next step is to lay the metadata, which is like a template, over the raw

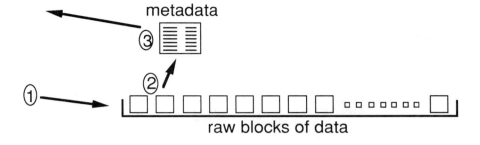

1 - the raw data is located
2 - the template - metadata - is
    laid over the raw data
3 - the "record" - including the raw
    data and its interpretation are
    returned to the programmer

Figure 6.3   Storing metadata as well as data.

data. Fields, keys, and physical characteristics of data are all now understood to the computer and to the program that has issued the READ. Now, the raw data is able to be interpreted. At this point the data is passed back to the programmer as a "record" or a "row" (or whatever unit of storage the programmer is used to).

Metadata has been around in one form or the other for as long as there have been computers. Even though metadata has been a passive "background" subject for many years, it takes on a new and vital importance in the client/server environment. It is the control of metadata that is the glue that holds together the client/server environment. Without a disciplined approach to metadata, one node in the client/server network cannot communicate and interface with another node, either for "corporate" client/server data or for node autonomous data that coincidentally is required by another node. Not only is metadata nec-

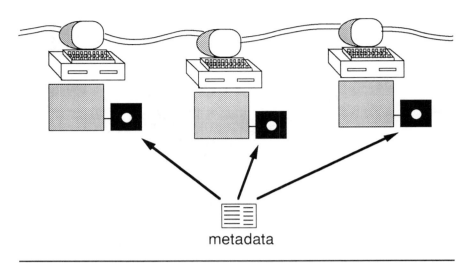

metadata

Figure 6.4   Common description for metadata—the key to
the control of metadata.

essary for simple communication between different nodes
in the client/server environment, but metadata is necessary for the establishment and control of the system of
record—for both the operational environment and the DSS
data warehouse environment.

Metadata, then, is a very important component of the
client/server environment. The role of metadata in the cli-
ent/server environment is shown in Figure 6.4.

There is a common definition of data structure for common data across the different nodes. Of course, the content of data, at least insofar as the system of record is
concerned, differs from node to node. But the structure
and content of common shared data across the nodes remains consistent. Because the structure of common data
remains consistent over the different nodes, code written
for one node is applicable and fully usable on other nodes,
as shown by Figure 6.5. Note that, for data solely used by
and understood by a single node, there is no need for a

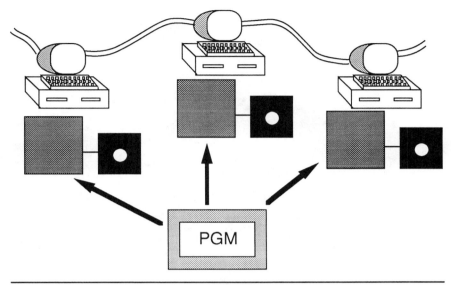

Figure 6.5   With a consistent definition of data, the same
code is applicable to multiple nodes.

common definition. Centralized metadata control is not
needed or even desirable for truly private data. But for
commonly used and controlled data, a metadata source
outside the nodes is needed.

If there were no control and discipline of metadata
across the client/server environment, then in short order
each node would have its own private structure of data
and, as a consequence, each node would have to have its
own tailored code. The result would be pure chaos across
the client/server environment.

CENTRAL REPOSITORY

In order to establish and maintain discipline across the
client/server environment, it is necessary to have a com-

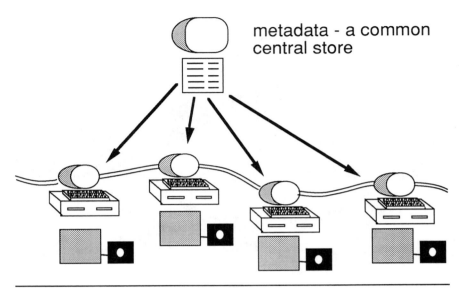

Figure 6.6   Managing the network.

mon or central repository of metadata for commonly shared data, as shown by Figure 6.6.

The central store should contain:

- information about the system of record, both operational and DSS
- data layouts, including
  keys
  attributes
  physical characteristics
  structure of attributes
  relationships between data structures
  attribute units of measurement
  encoding/decoding information
  encryption/decryption information
  compression/decompression information
  default information

      the relationship of the physical structure of data to
        the data model
- for the DSS system of record
     source data
     alias information
     extract information
     volumetrics
     integration information
     extract history
     current value to time variancy transformation
     versioning
     levels of granularity, compaction relationships, and
       purge criteria.

Of interest is not only what should go into the metadata repository but what should not go. In general, the following information does *not* go into the metadata central store:

- metadata for temporary or private files.

One of the primary issues in regard to the use of metadata is its accessibility. As a rule, the more accessible metadata is, the better. Conversely, the moment that metadata becomes difficult to access, the less its value. The only real restriction is on the changing of metadata, for which there needs to be a fairly strict discipline.

    The administration of metadata is a corporate function, a function that extends across all nodes in the client/server network. Usually the corporate database administrator is charged with management of metadata. One of the most important issues related to metadata is that of change control. In order to be effective, change control—not just of data, but of programs as well—must be administered evenly and synchronously across the network. Figure 6.7 illustrates the problems of change control.

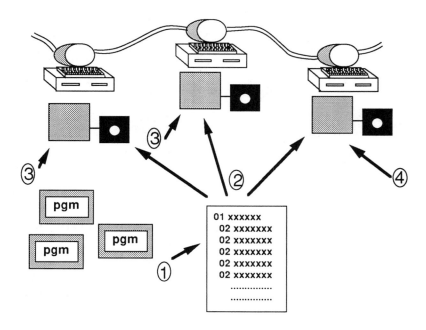

1 - changes made to data definition at moment n
2 - program, data changes are sent to nodes at
moment n + 1
3 - program, data changes are implemented
selectively at moment n + 2
4 - program, data changes are not implemented
by moment n + 3

Figure 6.7   Now the client/server network is out of synch.

In Figure 6.7 changes have been made to programs and
data. Some of the program and data changes are made at
the node level, but other changes are not made. The minute
that one part of the network considers a program to be in
one status and another part of the network considers a pro-

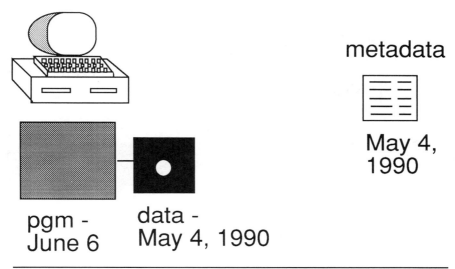

metadata

May 4, 1990

pgm - June 6

data - May 4, 1990

Figure 6.8   Time stamping at both the node level and the metadata level is necessary to keep the client/ server environment in synch.

gram to be in another status, the entire network is out of synch. A good practice to minimize problems (or at least help the environment stay in synch) is to time-stamp programs and code at both the node level and the metadata level, as shown by Figure 6.8.

Where there is a "pure" server environment, the server becomes a good place to house the metadata control software and administration.

SUMMARY

Metadata is data about data. It is an essential part of the control mechanism required for the client/server environment. In order to control corporate data, data and programs across the network, a central repository of metadata needs to be stored. Because nodes tend to get out of synch, maintaining a time stamp for programs and data at both the node level and the central repository level is a good design practice.

7

A Client/Server Development Methodology

Production is not the application of tools to materials,
but logic to work.

Peter Drucker

There is a universal appeal to development methodologies. Appealing to the intellect, a methodology purports to direct the developer down a rational path, pointing out what needs to be done, in what order, and how long the activity should take. Across the board, the enthusiasm for methodologies has met with disappointment upon implementation. The track record for methodologies—for the client/server environment or any other environment, for that matter—has been poor.

Why have development methodologies, in general, been a disappointment upon facing the reality of implementation? There are a plethora of reasons:

- Methodologies generally show a flat, linear flow of activities. In fact, almost any methodology requires execution in terms of iterations. In other words, it is absolutely normal to do two or three steps, stop, and repeat all or part of those steps again. Methodologies usually don't show or concern themselves with iterations of activities.
- Methodologies usually show activities as occurring once and only once. Indeed, some activities need to be done successfully only once. However, other activities are done repeatedly for different cases.
- Methodologies usually show a prescribed set of activities to be done. Often, some of the activities don't need to be done at all, while other activities need to be done that are not shown as part of the methodology.
- Methodologies often tell how to do something, not what needs to be done. In describing how to do something, the effectiveness of the methodology becomes lost in detail.
- Methodologies often do not distinguish between the sizes of the systems being developed under the methodology. Some systems are so small that a rigorous methodology makes no sense. Some systems are just the right size for a methodology. Other systems are so large that their sheer size and complexity will overwhelm the methodology.
- Methodologies often mix project management concerns with the design and development activities to be done. Usually project management activities should be kept separate from methodological concerns.
- Methodologies often do not make the distinction between operational and DSS processing. However, the system development life cycles for operational and DSS processing are diametrically opposed. In order to be suc-

cessful, there must be a clear distinction between operational and DSS processing.

- Methodologies often do not include checkpoints and stopping places in the case of failure. "What is the next step if the previous step has not been done properly?" is usually not a standard part of a methodology.
- Methodologies are often sold as solutions, not tools. When a methodology is sold as a solution, inevitably the methodology is asked to replace good judgment and common sense, and this is always a mistake.

Despite these drawbacks, there still is a general appeal for methodologies. A general-purpose methodology applicable to the client/server environment will be developed, in full understanding of the pitfalls of methodologies. The methodology for development in the client/server environment that is outlined owes much to its early predecessors. For a much fuller exploration of the intricacies and techniques described, refer to books on methodology listed in the references for this book.

A PHILOSOPHICAL OBSERVATION

In some regards, the best methodology around is that of the Boy and Girl Scout merit badge system. The merit badge system is used to determine when a scout is ready to pass on to the next rank. The merit badge system has stood the test of time. The merit badge system applies to both country dwelling and city dwelling boys and girls, as well as to athletically inclined and intellectually inclined children. The merit badge system applies to kids in the Southwest, California, Northeast, and Florida. In short, the merit badge system is a uniform methodology for the measurement of accomplishment. Is there any secret to the merit badge methodology? If there is any secret, it is this: The merit badge methodology does not prescribe *how* any activity is to be accomplished; it merely describes what is to be done. The "how" is up to the boy or girl scout. Philosophically, the approach to methodology for the client/server environment that will be described in this chapter takes the same perspective. The results of what must be accomplished will be described. What is required to achieve those results is left entirely up to the developer.

TWO METHODOLOGIES

First a methodology for operational systems and processing in the client/server environment will be described. Then a methodology for DSS systems and processing in the client/server environment will be described. Note that *NO!* methodology for node autonomous development will be described. The methodologies discussed are entirely for "corporate" client/server data and processing. Figure 7.1 graphically shows the general steps taken to develop a corporate operational client/server architecture.

The point of departure for discussing what methodology to use where is to start with the difference between operational processing and DSS processing. As a rule operational processing is processing that

- serves the clerical community,
- updates data,
- focuses on values contained in individual records,
- has programs that operate on relatively few records, and
- requires quick response time.

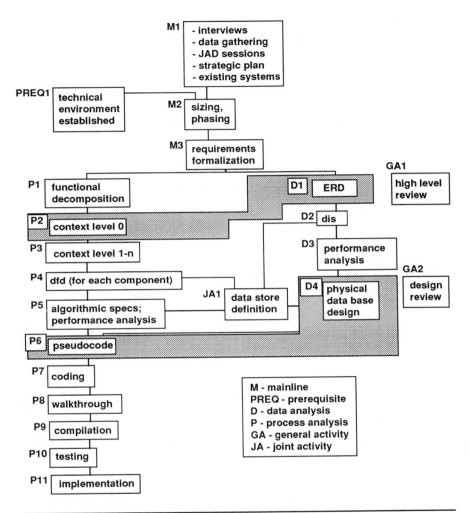

Figure 7.1   Operational development.

DSS processing is processing that

- serves the managerial community,
- accesses, calculates, and displays data, but does not update data,
- focuses on values that operate on many records, and
- requires relaxed response time.

OPERATIONAL CLIENT/SERVER SYSTEMS

M1—Initial Project Activities

- *Interviews*. The output of interviews is the "softcore" description of what the system is to do, usually reflecting the opinion of middle management. The format of the output is very free-form. As a rule, the territory covered by interviews is not comprehensive.
- *Data gathering*. The output from this activity may come from many sources. In general, requirements, usually detailed, are gathered here that are not caught elsewhere. This is a free-form, catchall, requirements-gathering activity, the results of which "fill in the gap" for other requirements-gathering activities.
- *JAD (Joint Application Design) session output*. The output from this activity(ies) is the group "brainstorm" synopsis. One of the benefits of requirements formulation in a JAD session is the spontaneity and flow of ideas, and the critical mass that occurs by having different people in the same room focusing on a common objective. The output of one or more JAD sessions is a formalized set of requirements that collectively represent the end-user's needs.
- *Strategic business plan analysis*. If the company has a strategic business plan, it makes sense to reflect on how the strategic business plan relates to the require-

ments of the system being designed. The influence of the strategic business plan can manifest itself in many ways—in setting growth figures, in identifying new lines of business, in describing organizational changes, and so forth. All of these factors, and more, shape the requirements of the system being built.

- *Existing systems shape requirements for a new system profoundly.* If related existing systems have been built, at the very least the interface between the new set of requirements and existing systems must be identified. Conversion, replacement, parallel processing, and so forth are all likely topics. The output from this activity is a description of the impact and influence of existing systems on the requirements for the system being developed.

M2—Sizing, Phasing

After the general requirements are gathered, the next step is to size them and divide development into phases. If the system to be developed is large, it makes sense to divide the system into small, manageable units. Of course, the different development phases must be organized into a meaningful sequence, so that the second phase builds on the first, the third phase builds on the first and second, and so forth. The output from this step is the breaking up of general requirements into more manageable phases, assuming the requirements are large enough to require a breakup at all.

M3—Requirements Formalization

Once the requirements have been gathered, sized, and phased (if necessary), the next step is to formalize them. In this step the developer ensures that

- the requirements that have been gathered are complete, insofar as it is reasonably possible to gather them,
- the requirements are organized,
- the requirements are not in conflict with each other,
- the requirements do not overlap, and
- that operational and DSS requirements have been separated.

The requirements include the identification of and the conformance to the service level agreement for the shop.

The output from this step is a requirements definition that is ready to go to detailed design.

PREQ1—Technical Environment Definition

In order to proceed, it is necessary to define the technical environment. Certain elements of design beyond this point depend on the identification of technical cornerstones. At the least, the following should be established:

- the hardware platform(s) to be used
- the operating system(s) to be used at each node
- the DBMS(s) to be used
- the network software to be used
- the language(s) to be used for development

In addition to a definition of what hardware, software, and networking will be used, it is helpful to have established the following as well:

- ring configuration/bridges between rings
- node residency
- management of the system of record
- network protocol/compatibility
- other general operating characteristics of the client/server environment

D1—ERD (Entity Relationship Diagram)

From the general set of formal requirements comes the need to identify the major subjects that will make up the system and the relationship of those major subjects. As a rule, a major subject of the enterprise is a collection of data which has been synthesized into the highest level of abstraction. Typical major subjects are CUSTOMER, PRODUCT, TRANSACTION, and so forth. The relationships of the major subjects are identified, as well as the cardinality. The output from this step is the identification of the major subjects that will make up the system, as well as the relationship of the subjects to one another.

D2—DIS (Data Item Sets)

Each subject is further broken down, in terms of level of detail, into a dis (data item set). This dis contains attributes of data, the grouping of attributes, and keys. In addition, "type of" data is identified. Other structures of data here include connectors—representations of relationships—and secondary groupings of data. The output from this step is the "fleshing-out" of the subject areas identified in D1.

D3—Performance Analysis

This step is performed if the volume of data, the volume of processing, the traffic over the network, the growth of data and processing, or the peak period of processing will produce significant amounts of activity. If none of those factors will occur, this step is not done.

In this step the issue of physical denormalization of data is addressed. Specifically, the design practices of

- introduction of derived data,
- merging tables,

- selective introduction of redundancy,
- creating arrays of data, and,
- further separation of data.

are considered. If this activity is done at all, the output reflects a much more streamlined design, with little or no loss of the benefits of normalization of data.

D4—Physical Database Design

Now the output from D3 and/or D4 is used to produce a physical database design. Some of the characteristics of the output include

- sequential ordering of data,
- indexing,
- physical attribution of data,
- designation of keys,
- clustering/interleaving,
- management of variable length data,
- NULL/NOT NULL specification,
- referential integrity, and so forth.

The output from this step is the actual specification of the database to the DBMS, or whatever data management software/conventions are adopted.

P1—Functional Decomposition

From the requirements document comes the functional decomposition. The functional decomposition merely takes the broad function accomplished by the system and breaks it down into a series of succeedingly smaller functions (down to a level sometimes called the "primitive" level). The output from this process is a large functional decomposition describing the different activities to be performed from a high level to a low level.

P2—Context Level 0

Context level 0 of the functional decomposition describes, at the highest level of abstraction, the major activities to be performed. Context level 0 corresponds to the ERD in data modeling.

P3—Context Level 1–*n*

The remaining levels of the functional decomposition describe the more detailed activities that occur. Context levels 1-*n* correspond in terms of process design to the data item set (the dis) in terms of data design.

P4—Data-Flow Diagram—(dfd)

At each context level *n*—the primitive level—a dfd is drawn. The dfd indicates the input to a process, the output from a process, the data stores needed to establish the process, and a brief description of the process. Data-flow diagrams may be done for context levels higher than *n* if it turns out that a program or process is likely to be written for that context level.

P5—Algorithmic Specification; Performance Analysis

The processes that are defined by the dfd are further broken down into a detailed algorithmic specification. In other words, in this step, the actual processing to occur is outlined.

In addition, if performance is to be an issue, the effect of performance on program design is factored in. Such design techniques as

- making sure the data is accessed and physically organized into a sequence that is efficient,
- breaking a long running program into a series of shorter running programs,
- requiring a program to access a smaller amount of nonnode resident data,
- shortening the time a unit of data is locked,
- changing a lock from update potential to access, and so forth,
- making sure work done before displaying data on a screen is not excessive

are considered here.

In addition the following need to be done for each module:

- Identify how often the module will be executed.
- Identify the peak periods of processing that will occur.
- Identify what data will be needed and how it will be structured.
- Identify the performance requirements of the module, especially if they are out of the ordinary.

P6—Pseudocode

The algorithms and program specifications are further refined into pseudocode. The designer ensures that all needed data for processing is available. All variables used in calculations, transformations, updates, and the like are identified here. Any loose ends are identified. The output from this activity is coding specifications ready for actual code.

P7—Coding

The pseudocode is translated into source code. If the data has been designed properly and if the pseudocode has been thorough, this step goes smoothly. The output from this step is source code.

P8—Walk-through

The walk-through is the verbal explanation of code in front of peers. The intent is to find errors before testing. The output from this step is code that has been publicly aired and is as free from error as possible.

P9—Compilation

Source code is run through the compiler. All errors found in compilation are corrected. The output from this step is compiled code, ready to be tested.

P10—Testing

Compiled code is tested. There are several levels of testing. The simplest (lowest) level of testing occurs when the compiled module is tested by itself, ensuring that the function it does is satisfactory. Next, the compiled code is added to other code with which the compiled code will have to work. New levels of testing occur in order to ensure the integration of the compiled code with other modules that will be interfaced. A third level of testing occurs when major groups of modules are ready to be tested together.

If there is a large volume of data and/or a significant amount of processing to be done, stress testing should be done as well. Stress testing entails forcing the system to perform as it would over peak periods of time or over peak volumes of data. As a rule, 25% more data and/or 25% more processing is used in the stress test than will occur during peak loads.

The output from this step is tested code, ready for execution.

P11—Implementation

There are many activities in implementation. To some extent implementation is an ongoing activity that has no end. Some of the typical activities of implementation are

- training, indoctrination,
- loading of resident nodes with programs,
- initial loading of data,
- conversions of data, if necessary,
- monitor utilities established,
- documentation written,
- recovery, reorganization procedures established, and so forth.

The output from this step (if in fact there really is an end to the step) is a satisfactorily running system.

JA1—Data Store Definition

Data store definition occurs as a result of both data design and process design. The results of data store definition are simple. A data store is adequately designed when

- all data referenced in the dfd are present, available, and efficiently accessible, and
- all data referenced in the dis are present, available, and efficiently accessible.

In other words, the data store definition represents the intersection of data needs from the dfd (process model) and the dis (data model).

The output from this step is a definition of the data store that satisfies both process and data design.

GA1—High-Level Review

The high-level review simply ensures that both data and process design are in synch at an early, high level. Such issues surface as the scope of the effort, the need to separate primitive and derived data and processing, the support of data needs by the process designer, the support of the process needs by the data designer, and so forth. The output from this step is a high-level design ready to proceed down data and process paths.

GA2—Design Review

This activity is one of the most important in the entire development process. Design review gives the developer the best chance to succeed by catching errors—of any kind, in code specification, in database design, etc.—prior to casting of the system into the concrete of application code. Prior to coding, changes may be made to the system relatively easily and inexpensively. After coding, changes to the system are difficult and expensive. Refer to the literature in the references as to specific procedures for executing design review. An essential part of the design review process is the visualization of the entire system, especially as the system relates to performance.

The output from this step is an assessment to management of the strengths and weaknesses of the design, and recommendations to improve the quality of the system.

DSS SYSTEM OF RECORD DEVELOPMENT

The development of the DSS component of the client/ server environment proceeds on an essentially different path from that of the operational component because, in general, processing requirements are not a part of the DSS system of record development. In this sense the DSS system of record development is truly a data-driven process. The first step in the development of the DSS system of record is that of developing and populating the DSS system of record. A methodology for doing that phase of development is shown by Figure 7.2.

It is worth noting in Figure 7.2 that some of the activities specified are one-time-only activities, and some are activities that will recur upon population of a new sector or subject area. Principally, DSS1, DSS2, DSS3, DSS4 and DSS6 are one-time activities. All other DSS activities need to be redone for each new subject area that is populated. The assumption is made that a data model has been created prior to the beginning of DSS development. If no data model has been created, then the DSS developer needs to back up and create one.

It is assumed that the technological environment (as described in the operational development methodology) has been established. If the technological environment has not been established, it needs to be.

DSS1—Data Model Analysis (a one-time activity)

At the outset, a data model needs to have been defined. The data model needs to have

- identified the major subject areas
- separated primitive from derived data
- for each subject area, identified
    keys
    attributes
    groupings of attributes
    relationships among groupings of attributes
    multiply occurring data
    "type of" data

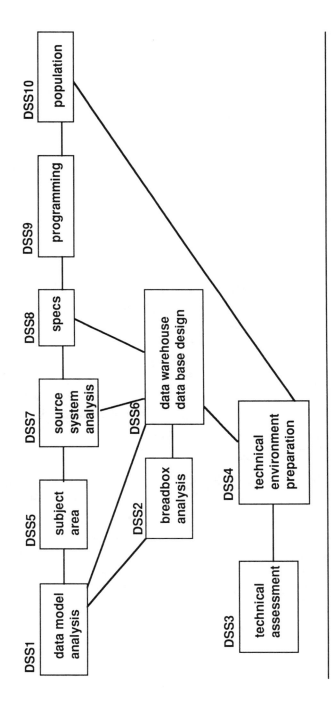

Figure 7.2 Warehouse development.

131

The output from this step is a confirmation that the organization has built a solid data model. If the model does not meet the criteria specified, then progress should be halted until the model is brought up to standards of quality.

DSS2—Breadbox Analysis (a one-time activity)

Once the model has been analyzed as brought up to a level of sufficient quality, the next step is to do "breadbox" analysis. Breadbox analysis is a sizing of the DSS environment in terms of gross estimates. If volume of data is going to be a problem, it is important to know at the outset. Breadbox analysis simply projects in raw terms how much data the DSS system of record—data warehouse—will hold. The output from breadbox analysis is simple—if the DSS system of record—data warehouse—is to contain large amounts of data, then multiple levels of granularity need to be considered. If the DSS system of record will not contain a massive amount of data, then there is no need to plan the design for multiple levels of granularity.

DSS3—Technical Assessment (a one-time activity)

The technical requirements for managing the DSS system of record—data warehouse—in the client/server environment are very, very different from the technical requirements and consideration for managing node residency of operational processing. A "pure" server works very well here. That is why a separate, central store of DSS data is so effective. The output from this step is a definition of how the DSS system of record is to be positioned across the client/server environment. The three most common choices are

- a central store available to but apart from the client/server network (such as a mainframe that functions as a server),

- a central store that is part of the client/server network (a "pure" server), or
- the distribution of the DSS system of record across the different nodes in the network (not a popular choice).

DSS4—Technical Environment Preparation (a one-time activity)

Once the architectural configuration for the DSS system of record has been established, the next step is to identify technically how the configuration can be accommodated. Some of the typical issues that much be addressed here are:

- What amount of DASD is required?
- What link—either across the client/server network, or into the client/server network—will be required?
- What volume of processing is anticipated?
- How can conflicts of processing between competing access programs be minimized and/or alleviated?
- What volume of traffic will be generated coming out of the technology that controls the DSS system of record—data warehouse?
- What is the nature of traffic—either short bursts or long bursts—coming out of the technology that controls the DSS system of record?

DSS5—Subject Area Analysis

Now the subject area to be populated for the data warehouse is selected. The first subject area to be selected must be large enough to be meaningful and small enough to be implementable. It usually helps to have the first subject area related to the finances of the enterprise. If by some chance a subject area is truly large and complex, a subset of the subject area may be chosen for implementation. The output from this step is a scope of effort in terms of a subject.

DSS6—DSS System of Record Design (a one-time activity)

The design of the DSS system of record—data warehouse—is based on the data model. Some of the characteristics of the ultimate design include

- an accommodation of the different levels of granularity, if indeed there are multiple levels of granularity,
- an orientation of data to the major subjects of the corporation,
- the presence of only primitive data and publicly derived data in the data warehouse,
- the absence of non-DSS data,
- time variancy of every record of data,
- physical denormalization of data where applicable (i.e., where performance warrants), and
- creation of data "artifacts" where relationships of data once in the operational environment are brought over to the DSS system of record—data warehouse.

The output from this step is a physical database design of the data warehouse. Note that not all of the data warehouse needs to be designed in detail at the outset. It is entirely acceptable to design the major structures of the data warehouse initially, then fill in the details at a later point in time.

DSS7—Source System Analysis

Once the subject to be populated is identified, the next activity is to identify the source data for the subject in the existing systems environment. It is absolutely normal for there to be a variety of sources of data for DSS data. It is at this point that the issues of integration are addressed. The following represents the issues to be addressed here:

- key structure/key resolution as data passes from the operational environment to the DSS environment
- attribution
  - what to do when there are multiple sources to choose from
  - what to do when there are no sources to choose from
  - what transformations, encoding/decoding, conversions, and the like must be made as data is selected for transport to the DSS environment
- how time variancy will be created from current value data
- structure—how the DSS structure will be created from the operational structure
- relationships—how operational relationships will appear in the DSS environment

The output from this step is the mapping of data from the operational environment to the DSS environment.

DSS8—Specifications

Once the interface between the operational and the DSS environment has been outlined, the next step is to formalize the interface in terms of program specifications. Some of the major issues here include:

- How do I know what operational data to scan?
  - Is the operational data time stamped?
  - Is there a "delta" file?
  - Are there system logs/audit logs that can be used?

Can existing source code and data structure be changed to create a "delta" file?

Do "before" and "after" image files have to be rubbed together?

- How do I know where to store the output, once scanned?

Is the DSS data preallocated, preformatted?

Is data appended?

Are updates in the DSS environment made?

The output from this step are the actual program specifications that will be used to bring data over from the operational environment to the DSS system of record.

DSS9—Programming

This step includes all the standard activities of programming, such as

- development of pseudocode,
- coding,
- walk-throughs, and
- testing, in its many forms.

DSS10—Population

This step entails nothing more than the execution of the DSS programs previously developed. The issues addressed here are such things as

- the frequency of population,
- purging populated data,
- "aging" populated data (i.e., running tallying summary programs),

- managing multiple levels of granularity, and
- refreshing living sample data, if in fact living sample tables have been built.

The output from this step is a populated, functional DSS system of record.

The third phase of development in the architected environment is the usage of DSS system of record data for the purpose of analysis. Once the data in the DSS system of record environment is populated, usage may commence.

There are several essential differences in the development that occurs at this level and development in other parts of the environment. The first major difference in development here is that the development process always starts with data, i.e., the data in the DSS system of record—data warehouse. The second difference is that requirements are not known at the start of the development process. The third difference (which is really a by-product of the first two factors) is that processing is done in a very iterative, very heuristic fashion. In other types of development, there is always a certain amount of iteration. But in the DSS component of development occurring after the DSS system of record—data warehouse—is developed, the whole nature of iteration changes. Iteration of processing is a normal and essential part of the analytical development process, much more so than it is elsewhere.

The steps taken in the DSS development components can be divided into two categories: the repetitively occurring analysis (or, as is sometimes called the "departmental" or "functional" analysis), and the true heuristic processing (or the "individual" level).

Figure 7.3 shows the steps to be taken after the DSS system of record—data warehouse—has begun to be populated.

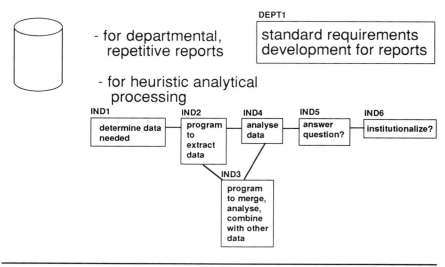

Figure 7.3   Heuristic development.

DEPT1—Repeat Standard Development

For repetitive analytical processing (usually called delivering standard reports) the normal requirements-driven processing occurs. This means that the following steps (described earlier) are repeated:

M1—interviews, data gathering, JAD, strategic plan, existing systems
M2—sizing, phasing
M3—requirements formalization
P1—functional decomposition
P2—context level 0
P3—context level 1–n
P4—dfd for each component
P5—algorithmic specification; performance analysis
P6—pseudocode

P7—coding
P8—walk-through
P9—compilation
P10—testing
P11—implementation

In addition, at least parts of the following will occur at the appropriate time:

GA1—high-level review
GA2—design review

It does not make sense to do the data-analysis component of development, because the developer is working from the DSS system of record. Reports that are produced on a regular basis comprise the output from this activity.

IND1—Determine Data Needed

At this point, data in the DSS system of record—data warehouse—is selected for potential usage in the satisfaction of reporting requirements. While the developer works from an educated guess perspective, it is understood that the first two or three times this activity is initiated only some of the data needed will be retrieved. The output from this activity is data selected for further analysis.

IND2—Program to Extract Data

Once the data for analytical processing is selected, the next step is to write a program to access and strip the data. The program written should be able to be modified easily because it is anticipated that the program will be run, modified, then rerun on numerous occasions.

IND3—Combine, Merge, Analyze

After data has been selected, next it is prepared for analysis. Often times this means

- editing the data,
- combining with other data,
- refining the data, etc.

Like all other heuristic processes, it is anticipated that this program will be written so that it is easily modifiable and able to be rerun quickly. The output from this activity is data fully usable for analysis.

IND4—Analyze Data

Once data has been selected and further prepared, the question is asked, "Do the results obtained meet the needs of the analyst?" If the results are not met, another iteration occurs. If the results are met, then the final report preparation is begun.

IND5—Answer Question

The final report produced is often the result of many iterations of processing. Very seldom is the final conclusion the result of a single iteration of analysis.

IND6—Institutionalization

The final issue to be decided is whether the final report that has been created should be institutionalized. If there is a need to run the report repetitively, it makes sense to submit the report as a set of requirements and to rebuild the report as a regularly occurring operation.

SUMMARY

This chapter has described a data-driven development methodology for the client/server environment in which the differing needs of operational processing and DSS processing are served. At the center of the methodology is the DSS system of record—data warehouse.

8

Database Design Issues in the Client/Server Environment

To be a success in business, be daring, be first, be different.

Marchant

Previous chapters have described basic aspects of the client/server environment, such as the need for node residency to be based on the topology of the organization being served, the differences between operational and DSS processing, and the need for the definition of the system of record. The previous chapter described a development methodology in which the different aspects of design were organized into a meaningful order. This chapter will describe some database design techniques that the developer in the client/server environment will find useful.

MANAGING PRIMITIVE AND DERIVED DATA

Primitive data is data whose existence depends on a single occurrence of a major subject. Derived data is data whose existence depends upon multiple occurrences of a major subject. All derived data has been calculated in one form or the other. (Interestingly, however, all calculated data is not derived.)

Some examples of primitive data (in a banking environment) are

- the date of a withdrawal,
- the amount of the withdrawal,
- the teller servicing the withdrawal,
- the identification used for the person making the withdrawal,
- the account the withdrawal is made from,
- the account balance prior to the withdrawal, and so forth.

In short, primitive data is data that is accurate up to the second, detailed, and used to drive the day-to-day activities of the corporation.

Derived data is data that is calculated, for the most part. For example, in the banking environment, the following are derived data:

- the average balance of all customers, right now,
- the moving average, over the past six months, of all the stop payments made on accounts with less than $500 in the account,
- the total number of accounts that have overdraft protections, and so forth.

(*Note:* the subject of primitive and derived is a much more complex subject than this short introduction makes it out to be. Of the data in the world, 95 percent is clearly either primitive or derived. The remaining 5 percent of the data in the world is not nearly so well-behaved. The handling of the 5 percent causes great, complex discussions to occur. For an in-depth treatment of primitive and derived data, refer to the book, *Data Architecture: The Information Paradigm,* (QED, 1988). The reason why we are concerned with primitive and derived data in database design is that derived data can be created faster than it can be modeled and designed. An analyst can create and destroy more derived data with Lotus 1-2-3 than the database designer can handle. Furthermore, the operational environment is almost exclusively made up of primitive data. And a further complicating factor is that there typically is a 20:1 ratio of derived data to primitive data.

Because of the volume and mutability of derived data, a sound design principle is that

- operational database design will not include derived data, and
- derived data will be managed exclusively by DSS processes beyond the DSS system of record.

RELATIONSHIPS IN THE CLIENT/SERVER ENVIRONMENT

One of the most useful aspects of a database is the capability to relate one unit of data to another unit of data. The relationship can sometimes be designed and managed within the confines of the system or DBMS software. In other cases the relationship must be supported at the application level. The first decision to be made, then, in building relationships between one unit of data and another is how the relationship is to be supported. The following table outlines some of the considerations in selecting how to support the relationship.

DBMS/System supported	*Application Supported*
• not always an option	• an option in every case
• utilities supplied	• utilities must be written
• limited structures supported	• any structure supported
• recovery options limited	• plenty of recovery options

The next decision to be made is exactly how to implement the relationship. Some examples will be used to describe the typical options. Suppose a supplier is able to supply a part. The relationship then is one-to-many from a residence to a phone number. John Smith's house is serviced by phones 555-1234 and 555-1256. Assuming that resident name is the key to the residence table, and phone number is the key to the phone table, the one-to-many relationship can be implemented as shown in Figure 8.1.

Note that in Figure 8.1 there is an index on residence/phone data such that going from residence to phone is easily accomplished. However, in the database design shown in the figure, going from phone to residence is an inefficient exercise. If it is desired to go from phone to residence, it is easy enough to add another index to the residence/phone table on phone number, as shown by Figure 8.2.

While the $1:n$ relationship occurs frequently, another equally occurring option is the $m:n$ relationship. In reality, an $m:n$ relationship is merely the combination of two relationships, a $1:n$ relationship and the converse of the relationships—an $m:1$ relationship. For example, suppose a part could have many suppliers and a supplier could supply many parts, a naturally occurring business phenomena, as shown by Figure 8.3.

Figure 8.3 shows parts ABC, BCD and CDE, suppliers Jones, K-Mart, Emporium, and Bailey's, and several oc-

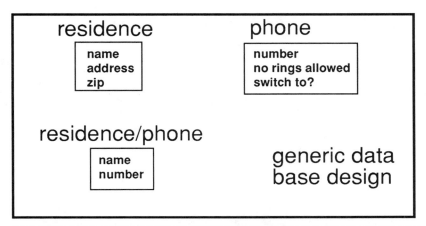

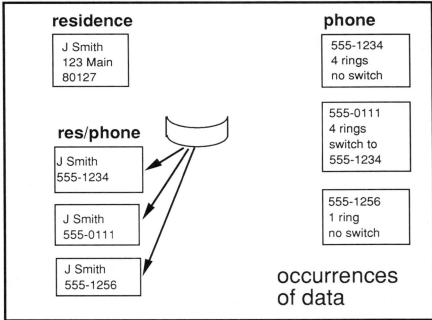

Figure 8.1   Generic design and occurrences of data.

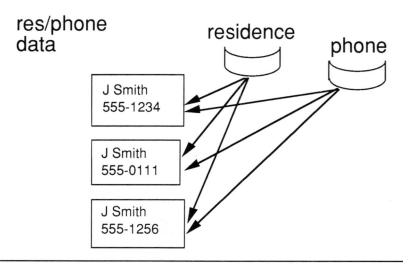

Figure 8.2   An index by phone number as well as residence.

currences of the relationships between part and supplier. The figure shows that ABC is supplied by Jones, K-Mart, and Baileys, BCD is supplied by Jones, and CDE is supplied by Jones, Baileys, and K-Mart. Looking at the relationship from the suppliers' perspective, Jones supplies ABC, BCD, and CDE, K-Mart supplies ABC and CDE, Emporium does not supply anyone, and Baileys supplies ABC and CDE.

Of course, it is possible for the intersection data, i.e., part/supplier data, to have its own data. Suppose that an intersection record were created each time a shipment was made from a supplier, as shown in Figure 8.4.

Figure 8.4 shows that shipments are recorded by date, part, and supplier. On Sept. 12, a shipment of ABC was made from Jones. On Sept. 16, a shipment was made by Jones of ABC. On Sept. 16, a shipment of BCD from the Emporium was made. On Sept. 12, a shipment of BCD by Jones was made, and so forth. Note that in order to

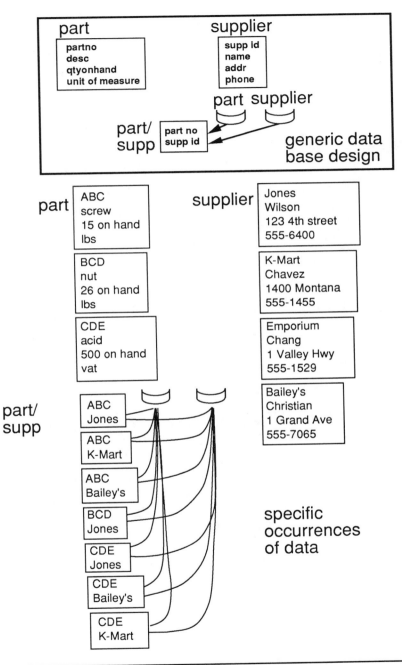

Figure 8.3 Different occurrences of part, supplier, and part/supplier data.

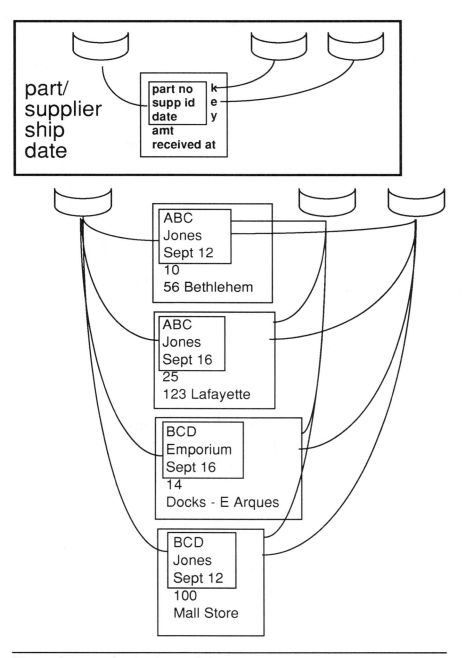

part/ supplier ship date

part no	key
supp id	
date	
amt	
received at	

ABC
Jones
Sept 12
10
56 Bethlehem

ABC
Jones
Sept 16
25
123 Lafayette

BCD
Emporium
Sept 16
14
Docks - E Arques

BCD
Jones
Sept 12
100
Mall Store

Figure 8.4   Occurrences of data.

achieve uniqueness, the full key—partno, supp id, and date—is required. If more than one shipment per day for the same part from the same supplier can be made, it may be necessary to make date/time the key, in order to ensure uniqueness of keys.

Note that nothing more than tables and indexes are required to build 1:*n* and *m*:*n* relationships. These relationships may be built at the application level in any case. In some technologies that run on client/server software these relationships can be built and supported.

As a rule, the key structure for any and every table in the client/server environment will include reference to the field over which node residency is delineated. In other words, if a client/server network were delineated by geography, the database design for the part/supplier relationship as shown would look like Figure 8.5.

Figure 8.5 shows that each table's key is preceded by region, where region is used to delineate node residency.

```
┌─────────────────────────┐     ┌─────────────────┐
│ REGION                  │     │ REGION          │
│ PART NO                 │     │ SUPP ID         │
│ DESC                    │     │ NAME            │
│ QTYONHAND               │     │ ADDR            │
│ UNITOFMEASURE           │     │ PHONE           │
└─────────────────────────┘     └─────────────────┘


      ┌─────────────┐
      │ REGION      │
      │ PART NO     │
      │ SUPP ID     │
      └─────────────┘
```

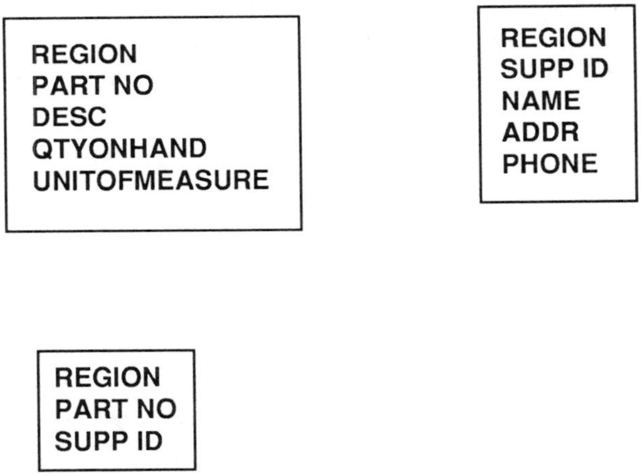

Figure 8.5   Each table's key structure has a prefix of region, where region is used to delineate node residency.

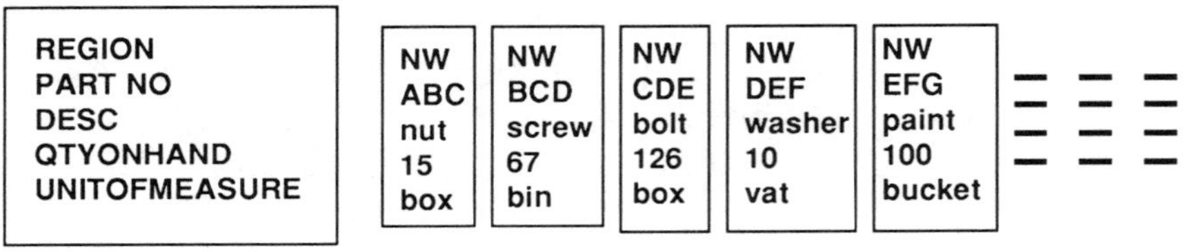

| REGION
PART NO
DESC
QTYONHAND
UNITOFMEASURE | NW
ABC
nut
15
box | NW
BCD
screw
67
bin | NW
CDE
bolt
126
box | NW
DEF
washer
10
vat | NW
EFG
paint
100
bucket | — — —
— — —
— — —
— — — |

Figure 8.6 For the northwest node, all values of the field—REGION—will equal "NW."

The argument can be made, why put region as a leading part of the key? After all, all data residing in a node will have the same region designation, as shown by Figure 8.6.

It is true that the same data (in the case shown, "NW") will be duplicated throughout the node. However, when another node wishes to access data from the NW node, it will be clear what node the data belong to. By the same token, when data is brought into the NW node from the southeast ("SE"), it will be clear that the NW node can do what it wishes to with the data, as long as it recognizes the data has come from and belongs to another node's residency.

INDEXING

The normal method of accessing data in a node is through an index. A simple arrangement of indexes and data is shown by Figure 8.7.

In Figure 8.7, an index, sequenced on the key "supplier id," points to the data in the node, residing on hard disk. The index is a fast way to get at a single record of data. Without the index, looking for even a single record would require a scan of the entire supplier table. Indexes then, increase the efficiency of access of data.

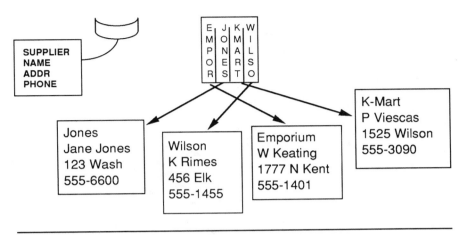

Figure 8.7   An index and primary data.

There is a downside to indexes, however. Whenever an update deletion or creation of a record occurs, the index must likewise be updated. An example of the overhead activity for indexes is shown by Figure 8.8.

Because indexes require the overhead of maintenance (not to mention the amount of space that an index requires), there is a trade-off the designer makes in the client/server environment. The designer makes the trade-off between efficient access of data and efficient update of data. If data is frequently accessed but seldom updated, then the designer probably will specify many indexes. If the data is frequently updated but seldom accessed, then the designer will specify very few indexes. The following rule of thumb applies:

Heavy Update/ *Limited Access*	*Heavy Access/* *Limited Update*
1–2 indexes	8–10 indexes

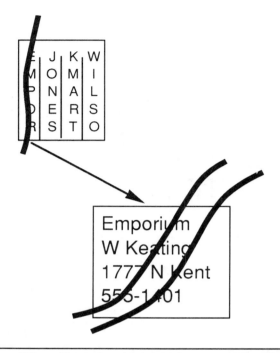

Figure 8.8   When Emporium is deleted as a supplier, the
index pointing to Emporium must be likewise
deleted.

But there are other considerations of indexes as well. The
physical organization of an index is important to performance. Figure 8.9 shows an index that has been created
and loaded at moment n.

Over time, many entries are added to the index, as
shown by the index at moment m. By this time, the physical organization of the index is very much in disarray. It
makes sense to either reorganize the index or to delete,
then recreate, the index in order to improve performance.
If the index shown at moment m is not physically restruc-
tured, every program that has to use the index pays the
penalty of overhead each time the index is used.

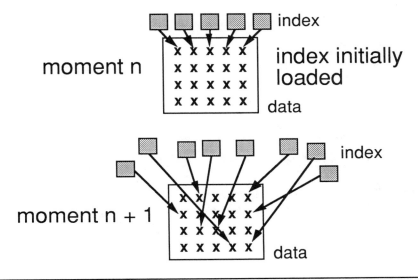

Figure 8.9   The index after many entries have been loaded—very disorganized.

Resequencing data through an index may also present a problem if much massive, sequential processing is occurring in the node. Consider the employee/education database shown in Figure 8.10. There are two indexes on the simple table. One index is on employee name; the other is on the school the employee attended. The index on employee name matches the physical sequencing of the data as the data is physically loaded onto hard disk.

If a full index scan must be done, it is much, much more efficient to scan the table by means of employee name than it is by school. Each access of data by school requires that a new location on hard disk be sought. Each access of data by name does not require that a new location on hard disk be sought. If an index is to be used to access large amounts of data, the physical ordering of the data should be considered.

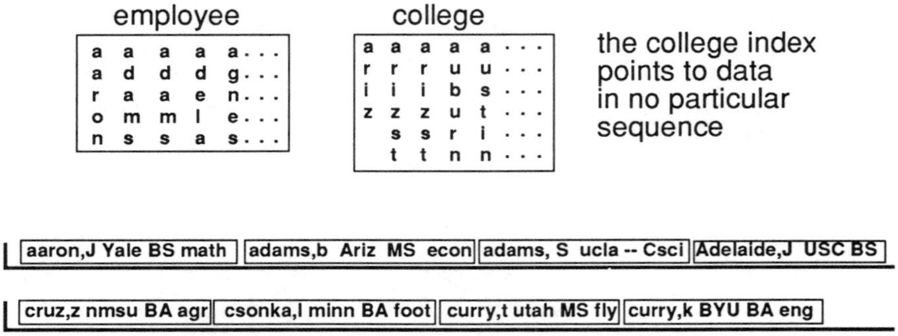

employee

```
a  a  a  a  a...
a  d  d  d  g...
r  a  a  e  n...
o  m  m  l  e...
n  s  s  a  s...
```

college

```
a  a  a  a  a...
r  r  r  u  u...
i  i  i  b  s...
z  z  z  u  t...
      s  s  r  i...
      t  t  n  n...
```

the college index
points to data
in no particular
sequence

| aaron,J Yale BS math | adams,b Ariz MS econ | adams, S ucla -- Csci | Adelaide,J USC BS |

| cruz,z nmsu BA agr | csonka,I minn BA foot | curry,t utah MS fly | curry,k BYU BA eng |

Figure 8.10   The physical order of the data in the primary
data area matches the order of the employee
index.

Another consideration of indexes is that some fields
should never be indexed. For example, consider Figure
8.11.

Figure 8.11 shows that gender points into an employee
table. The field, gender, has only two values, F or M. If a
field can have only a few values, it is more efficient to scan
the entire table than it is to use the index for access into
the table.

A final consideration of indexes in designing a client/
server database is the data over which the index will be
based. As a rule the data can be unique or nonunique, and
the data can be a single column or multiple columns. The
possibilities of index specification are

- unique, single column,
- unique, compound columns,
- nonunique, single column, and
- nonunique, compound columns.

an index on gender

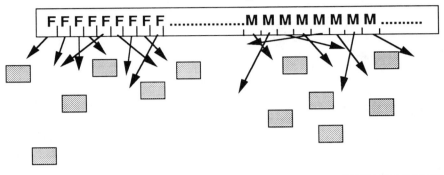

Figure 8.11   An employee table that is being indexed on gender.

DATA PARTITIONING

One of the most important topics of database design in the client/server environment is that of partitioning of data. Partitioning of data refers to the ability to break large databases up into distinct and separate physical units. Each partition-of-data unit shares the same structural definition but contains different data from other units. It is by means of data partitioning that data can be spread across different nodes and that node residency can be defined.

The reason why the subject of partitioning is so important a database design topic in the client/server world is that the database designer needs to select a partitioning strategy so that future partitions can be defined with minimal disruption to code serving the nodes. For example, on day one, there are four nodes—a North West (NW) node, a North East (NE) node, a South West (SW) node, and a South East (SE) node. When partitioning has been done properly, on day two there is no problem splitting the South West node into three separate nodes—a West Coast node, a Mountain States node, and a Central South node. When partitioning has been done properly, there is no disruption to existing code when the split is made.

ENCODING/DECODING DATA

A database design practice that deserves attention is that of encoding/decoding data. A simple example of encoding/decoding is "F" for female and "M" for male. Or "CO" for Colorado, "NY" for New York, "CA" for California, and so forth. Used properly, encoding can save space and I/O; used improperly, encoding can cause complications and can cost I/O's.

As long as the encoding scheme is obvious and easy to implement, encoding usually makes sense, but when it becomes complex and difficult to maintain, it usually is not a good design technique. When there must be constant interaction from the encoded value to the decoded value, then much I/O results, and encoding is not a sound practice. A special consideration of encoding/decoding in the client/server environment is that of keeping the decoded values across the nodes in synch. Just like programs and metadata, encoded values need to be time-stamped at each node and at the source, in order to resolve problems when the decoded values get to be out of synch.

VARIABLE-LENGTH DATA

Most DBMS that run in the pc/workstation environment allow data to be defined in terms of variable lengths. Variable-length data allows for the vast difference in occurrences of a field to be accommodated. For example, suppose a designer has specified for an employee file the field NAME. One occurrence of name is "Joe Lam," which consumes seven bytes. Another occurrence of name is "Stanislav Wiorkowsky," which consumes twenty bytes. If the name field is defined as fixed in length at twenty bytes, then the storage of "Joe Lam" wastes considerable space, as do all short names. Allowing a field to be variable in length can save lots of space, in the right circumstance.

There is a problem with variable-length data, however. When variable-length data can be updated, then there is a potential for a real space-management dilemma. For example, suppose the name field for "Kathy Allan" is to be updated, as shown in Figure 8.12.

In Figure 8.12 Kathy Allan has her record retrieved. She has recently married James Simpson and wishes to take her husband's name. To do so requires changing "Allan" to "Simpson," an addition of 2 bytes. The programmer makes the changes innocently enough. However, when it comes time to replace the variable data back into the location in which it originally fit, if the data is packed tightly, it won't fit, even though only two bytes have been added. The choice then becomes to place the record for Kathy Simpson in another physical location (thus interrupting the original sequence of the data and causing the indexes pointing into Kathy's record to be updated) or to split the data in the block to make space for Kathy's record. When the block of data is split, a new block with adequate space is found, and all the blocks that have been moved must have all their index entries adjusted to their new location. No wonder that variable-length data, if allowed to be updated, can cause a performance nightmare.

Another design issue for variable-length data has to do with the placement of variable-length fields in the record.

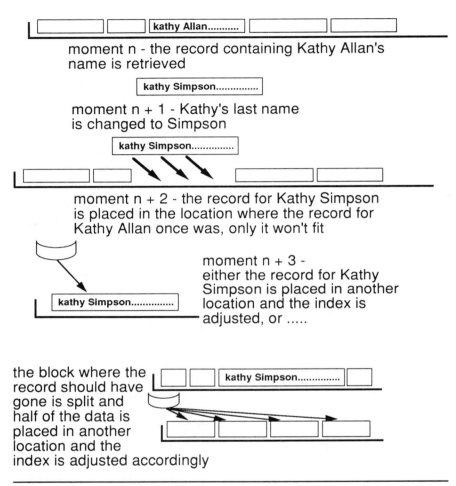

Figure 8.12   Space management and update.

As a rule, variable-length fields should be placed at the back of the record, with fixed-length fields at the front of the record. The reason for this is that determining the boundaries of the fixed-length field can be done independently of the length of the variable field(s). When fixed-length data is placed after variable-length data, then independence of field positioning is not possible.

EMBEDDED KEY INFORMATION

Choosing key structuring is very important. As a rule of thumb, the key structure should be random. In other words, there should be little or no embedded structural information in the key. Once the database designer allows embedded information to find its way into the key structure, code that accesses the key begins to be tied very closely to the data. When code begins to be closely tied to data, complexity of development and complexity of maintenance ensue.

RECURSION

Since this subject is very complex, only the highlights will be addressed here. The reader is advised that a much more detailed treatment of recursion is to be found in the book *DB2: Maximizing Online Performance in the Production Environment* (QED, 1988). Recursion occurs when an object has a relationship to itself. A common occurrence of recursion is the bill of materials, where one part relates to another part, until the final assembly is constructed. Recursion must be handled very carefully, because of the complexity that ensues if it is not handled properly. Unlike almost all other aspects of database design, in which there are many options to accomplish the desired result, with recursion there is only one correct way to design (for the general case) a database, as shown in Figure 8.13. There are four tables: a base table (containing standard part data), a "down" table (showing the

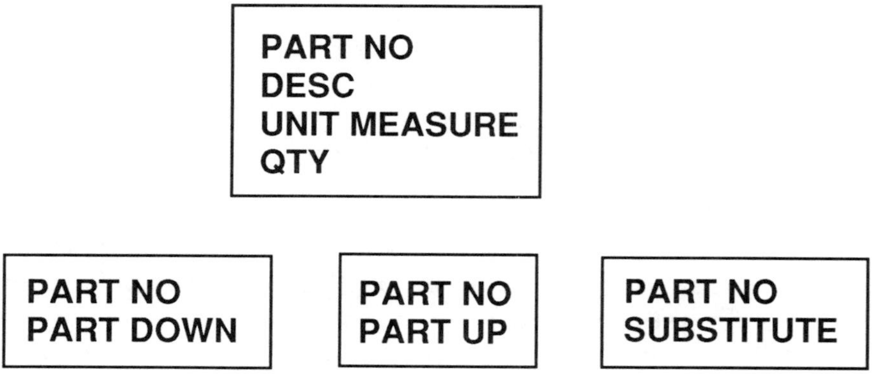

```
┌─────────────────────────┐
│  PART NO                 │
│  DESC                    │
│  UNIT MEASURE            │
│  QTY                     │
└─────────────────────────┘
```

```
┌──────────────────┐  ┌──────────────────┐  ┌──────────────────┐
│  PART NO          │  │  PART NO          │  │  PART NO          │
│  PART DOWN        │  │  PART UP          │  │  SUBSTITUTE       │
└──────────────────┘  └──────────────────┘  └──────────────────┘
```

Figure 8.13   The four tables that constitute the generic database design for a recursive structure.

relationship from a part to its subassembly), an "up" table, a part, and its substitute.

MICRO/MACRO VISION OF THE SYSTEM

In order for the client/server system to function in an optimal manner, it is necessary to view the system from both a "micro" and a "macro" perspective. The micro perspective looks at

- the interface of one technology to another,
- the detail design of data/programs,
- code,
- the flow of data from node to node, external storage to internal storage, and internal storage to the screen, and
- the indexing of data, and so forth.

The macro perspective of data looks at

- how all the parts of the system fit together,
- total system workload—peak periods, peak volumes, etc.,

- total system capacity, and
- functionality, etc.

There needs to be *both* a micro and a macro understanding of the client/server system in order for the system design to be successful. The micro perspective is part of the day-to-day design and development part of the environment. The macro perspective surfaces during the design review process, although it needs to be documented as part of the development of the system.

SUMMARY

In this chapter some basic database design issues have been addressed:

- primitive and derived data,
- relationships,
- indexing,
- partitioning,
- management of variable-length data,
- embedded key information, and
- recursion.

9

Program Design in the Client/Server Environment

If you steal from one author, it's plagiarism; if you steal from many it's research.

Wilson Mizner

In many ways program design in the client/server environment is very similar to program design in other environments. The principles of good program design change little from the client/server to any other environment. Still there are some twists that do occur because of the structure of the client/server environment. The following is an eclectic collection of programming practices, all of which are applicable to the client/server environment, some of which are applicable only to the client/server environment.

PROGRAM SEPARATION BY ENVIRONMENT

It is very important for the programmer to identify the particular environment in which he or she is building a program within the client/server environment because the structure, usage, orientation, code, and so forth all change from one environment to the next. Figure 9.1 shows that there are two major ways that programs are categorized in the client/server environment.

One important category is that of common code across all nodes versus node autonomous processing. The second important category is that of DSS versus operational pro-

	common code across all nodes	node autonomous
operational	- repeatable - node insensitive - performance oriented - supporting current value data - requirements driven - stringent documentation - standards across all nodes	- repeatable - node sensitive - performance oriented - supporting current value, node resident data - requirements driven, across the node - stringent documentation - standards within the node only
DSS	- non repeatable - node insensitive - not performance oriented - supporting time variant data - data driven; requirements unknown - stringent documentation - standards across all nodes	- non repeatable - node sensitive - not performance oriented - supporting node resident, time variant data - node resident data driven; requirements unknown - lax documentation - very few standards at all

Figure 9.1   Different characteristics of code over the different classifications of client/server processing.

cessing. Together the two categories form a matrix as shown by Figure 9.1.

Each cell in the matrix has its own unique characteristics. In the common code/operational cell, programs are repeatable. In this environment the client/server environment achieves its highest degree of leverage. The same program is run over and over, but on different data. The requirements that shape processing in this node are known and are gathered across all nodes. Stringent documentation is required for programs falling into this cell, as well as tight control of program load dates. The code that is written is insensitive to the node in which the program is being executed. Program performance in this category is an issue. Poor performance will manifest itself as a systems issue. The programs in this cell operate almost exclusively on current value data. A high degree of standardization across all nodes (not surprisingly!) is required. The code that is produced is documented stringently.

The cell that contains common code for DSS processing shares some of the characteristics of the cell for operational/common code. In this cell, DSS processing is done across all nodes, either producing an analytical result across the corporation or gathering data into a DSS system of record for further analysis. Some of the salient characteristics of programs found in this cell are as follows: Code generally is not repeatable (although there are some notable exceptions, in the case of regularly scheduled reports and extraction of data to the DSS system of record). The programs written for this cell are node insensitive. The requirements that shape processing are, for the most part, unknown (as is the case for all DSS processing). The programs written are in support of heuristic processing. The documentation that occurs here usually is stringent (at least in terms of DSS processing).

The next cell to be discussed is the node autonomous/ operational cell. Here, operational processing occurs that is applicable only to the node running the program. Because of the insularity of the programs in this cell, programming conventions that allow communications across the network do not have to be followed. Note that moving programs from this cell to other cells in the future could be a difficult thing to do. Data, programming conventions, stored modules, etc., are not standard across the network for this type of processing.

The final cell is the node autonomous/DSS cell. In this cell heuristic processing is found that is applicable only to the node. This cell is free form in every sense. Processing is nonrepeatable, in support of heuristic analysis. Programs are node sensitive. The requirements for processing are not known at the start of analysis, and so forth.

UNDERSTAND THE CELLS

It is vital that the programmer understand which cell his or her program is being written for because

- the programming practices differ drastically from one cell to the next, and
- generally speaking, a program written for one cell cannot be moved to another cell at a later point in time.

For these reasons, the programmer first must understand what cell the program is written for, then must understand what the conventions/standards are for that cell. If the programmer does not understand these concepts, why they are important, and how they apply, then very little else in the way of program practices matters.

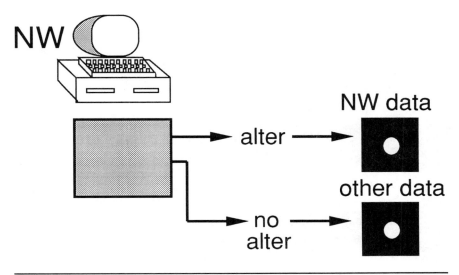

NW data

other data

Figure 9.2   The NW node can alter data that belongs to it,
but cannot alter other data that happens to be in
the node.

RESPECT FOR NODE RESIDENCY

Any data whose system of record lies outside a node cannot be changed, as shown by Figure 9.2. In the figure, all data node-resident to the NW node can be altered. All data not node-resident to the NW node cannot be altered.

A simple coding practice might look like

```
IF NODERES.DATA = NODERES THEN
UPDATE DATA.
```

In other words, from a coding perspective, before any update of data can be made, the data must be node-resident.

NODE SENSITIVITY/INSENSITIVITY

Code is node-sensitive when the code runs one way at one node and another way at another node. Code is node-insensitive when it runs the same way at all nodes. As a simple example of node sensitivity/insensitivity, consider the following code

```
IF NODERES.DATA = 'SW'
THEN ...
```

where NODERES equals the value of the node residence. In this case, the code is node-sensitive because it will run one way in the SW node, and differently in any other node. Now suppose the preceding code were written

```
IF NODERES.DATA = NODERES
THEN ...
```

If the node is the NW node, then NODERES = 'NW'. If the node is the SW node, then NODERES = 'SW', and so forth. In this case, the value of node residency is represented by a variable and is not hard-coded. This coding practice leads to node insensitivity, which is a good practice for common code across the network.

A strong argument for node insensitivity for common code is that future nodes can be added to the network with little or no impact on code.

PERFORMANCE

Where performance is an issue (i.e., in the common code/operational environment), some coding practices are:

- Make sure that code that has already executed does not have to be re-executed, if at all possible,
- Break long-running programs into a series of shorter running programs.
- Create programs that are parameter driven rather than using word coded variables.
- Checkpoint long-running programs.
- Monitor long-running programs to see how long they take to run, how many resources they use, etc.
- Use as few I/O's as possible.
- Do not allow a screen to be displayed with more data ready for display than what can be handled by a single screen,
- Schedule long-running programs to run when the network is least used.
- Take advantage of buffering of data whenever possible.
- Keep commonly used subroutines/modules in memory.
- Pass commonly used data as a parameter, rather than having each module reaccess the same data.

Performance across the network is achieved as a result of many design factors, not just program design. Database design, proper definition of node residency, expandability of the network, and so forth all contribute to performance as well as program design.

STANDARDIZATION

The need for (and the opportunity for) standardization is common throughout the client/server environment. The need for standardization of metadata has already been discussed in a previous chapter. Some (but hardly all!) of the considerations of standardization will be discussed here:

- Time-stamping of common code. The date/time of installation of common code will be kept at each node and at the point of metadata/common code storage. In the eventuality that common code gets out of synch across the network (over time, a very high probability), the usage of time stamps is invaluable in getting the applications running across the network back in synch.
- Nonrepeatability of code. Every unit of code must be unique. If the same unit of code appears in more than one place, then a common module must be created or logic rearranged in order not to have duplicate code created. (This practice is the so-called "code normalization" practice.) At the end of the day, all blocks or units of code will be unique.
- Each module will represent a unique and separate function.

SUMMARY

In summary, in this chapter we have discussed program design for the client/server environment. The first consideration of program design is an understanding of the environment the program is being built for. The client/server environments greatly shape the way that programs are built.

The second major program design issue is that of node sensitivity. Code that runs the same in any node is node insensitive. Code that runs differently from one node to the next is node sensitive. As a rule, unless there is a very strong reason for it, node insensitive code is the best policy.

Performance is another design concern for programs. The length of time a program runs, the length of time a unit of data is locked, the scheduling of programs, etc. are all important to the design of code in the client/server environment.

Other design issues include standardization of code, time stamping of code, and so forth.

Administration of the Client/Server Environment

Writing is the only profession where no one considers you ridiculous if you earn no money.

Jules Renard

There are two aspects of the client/server environment that make the job of administration even more important than in larger environments—the desire for autonomy at each node (which must be balanced against the need for control of "corporate" data and common code) and the size of the network, which is considerably smaller than the mainframe environment. Because of the smallness of size of networks in the client/server environment, administration is proportionately larger than the budget for administration is in larger environments. Administration then, is a very important component in the success of the client/server environment. There are two major aspects that must be administered: the network itself and the metadata and common code that support the "corporate" aspects for the client/server environment.

NETWORK ADMINISTRATION

Network administration involves the following tasks

- adding new nodes,
- bringing up, shutting down the network, assisting backup, problem shooting when errors occur,
- monitoring traffic, hotspots, queues, etc.,
- planning capacity, and
- interfacing with other networks; interfacing with the mainframe environment.

"CORPORATE" METADATA, COMMON CODE ADMINISTRATION

The second administrative function is that of administering the "corporate" aspects of the client/server environment, including metadata and common code. This aspect of administration is much more complex than network administration because it

- involves a large audience—developers, users, operators, managers, etc., across the network, and
- much of the administration of "corporate" aspects is at odds with the autonomy of processing at each of the nodes, which is one of the driving forces for client/server processing in the first place.

The two standard components to be administered are shown by Figure 10.1.

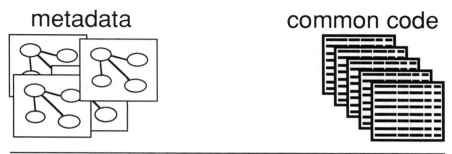

Figure 10.1   The standard components that need administration in the client/server environment.

The types of information that are in a corporate "library" are metadata and common code. Metadata includes

- the structure of data, including attributes, keys, physical characteristics, structure of attributes, and the interrelationships of one group of data to another;
- the time each structure of data has "gone live";
- the higher data model from which corporate data has been derived;
- the identification of the DSS system of record—data warehouse; and
- the identification of the source of DSS system of record—data warehouse (in other words, what extract processing was done to create data in the DSS system of record—data warehouse).

Keeping track not only of what the current status of metadata is, but also of changes over time may be useful as well. For example, suppose on April 15 the "corporate" definition of a data layout is changed, as shown in Figure 10.2. Knowing what changes have occurred over time,

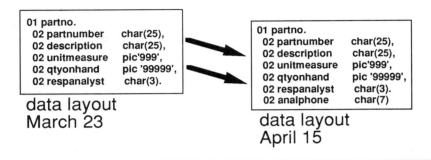

data layout
March 23

data layout
April 15

Figure 10.2   Tracking changes in metadata.

and when they occurred, can be as important as keeping a record of what is in effect at any moment in time.

In addition to classical metadata, another important facet that should be administered centrally is that of encoding/decoding and the use of common tables. Figure 10.3 shows that the encoded value of marketing districts has changed as of August 20.

Both values before and after need to be kept. The "after" values will be actively used. The "before" values will be archived so that future archived analysis will have a basis of data to turn to. This archiving of changed values is just one more task of the "corporate" client/server administration.

Besides metadata, the second major charge of the administration is that of common code. Common code is code that is spread over different nodes. Over time, maintenance occurs to existing code, new code is added, and old code is retired. It is the job of the administrator to ensure that there is only one "official" set of code in force at any one time, and to ensure that when changes to code are made, they are made uniformly across the nodes. In addition, when the code in the network gets out of synch, it is up to the administrator to lead the effort to get the node back in synch.

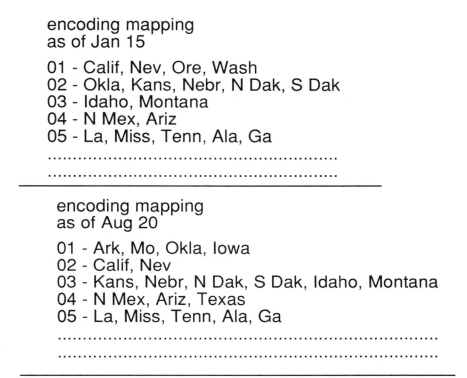

encoding mapping
as of Jan 15

01 - Calif, Nev, Ore, Wash
02 - Okla, Kans, Nebr, N Dak, S Dak
03 - Idaho, Montana
04 - N Mex, Ariz
05 - La, Miss, Tenn, Ala, Ga

encoding mapping
as of Aug 20

01 - Ark, Mo, Okla, Iowa
02 - Calif, Nev
03 - Kans, Nebr, N Dak, S Dak, Idaho, Montana
04 - N Mex, Ariz, Texas
05 - La, Miss, Tenn, Ala, Ga

Figure 10.3   On August 20 the marketing territories for a company
are changed by management decree. The business
changes are reflected in the encoding/decoding
structures that programmers employ.

Another function of the administrator is in assisting in
the development process (i.e., development for the "corporate" environment). The administrator's goal here is to
see that the basic building blocks of the systems are used
properly. This means

- ensuring that data already in existence is not rebuilt,
- ensuring that code already in existence is not rebuilt,
  and

- ensuring that current development efforts do what is needed to prepare for future development efforts.

Testing is another aspect of the administrator's job. The administrator is not charged with testing, per se, but the administrator *is* responsible for ensuring that data and programs put into production and made "official" have been tested.

Monitoring is yet one more task of the administrator. The types of monitoring include

- monitoring code and metadata time stamps at each node to ensure that the right versions are being used,
- monitoring data volume and usage across the network,
- monitoring machine usage and state of "busyness" across the network, etc.

The administrator sounds the early warning signal for any problems as they start to arise.

Training and indoctrination to the network and the technical environment are yet another component of the administrator's job. One of the most important tasks of the administrator is that of defining node residency and the monitoring of processing to ensure that the boundaries of node residency are not being violated. Interface to the mainframe environment and to other networks from the standpoint of "how to" is also a part of the administrator's job.

SUMMARY

One of the most important components of the client/server network is that of administration. Two nodes are required—network administration and the administration of "corporate" aspects of the client/server environment. Some of the aspects of "corporate" administration include

- managing metadata,
- managing common code,
- ensuring proper testing has occurred,
- monitoring the system,
- defining node residency, and
- training, indoctrination.

Client/Server, Mainframe Processing

One of the most important issues of the client/server environment, if there is to be reconcilability and order of data, is that of maintaining the DSS system of record. This issue is especially important in retrieving data from the mainframe environment. There are three possibilities shown.

In case 1, the mainframe environment has no data warehouse. In this case data is brought into the DSS system of record in the client/server environment from the mainframe environment, then released to the node for processing.

In case 2, there is a data warehouse in the mainframe environment. The data can be sent to the node for processing, with no need to go to the DSS system of record.

In case 3, there is a data warehouse. For reasons known to the client/server analyst, data is used from the warehouse, placed in the DSS system of record, then shipped to the node for processing.

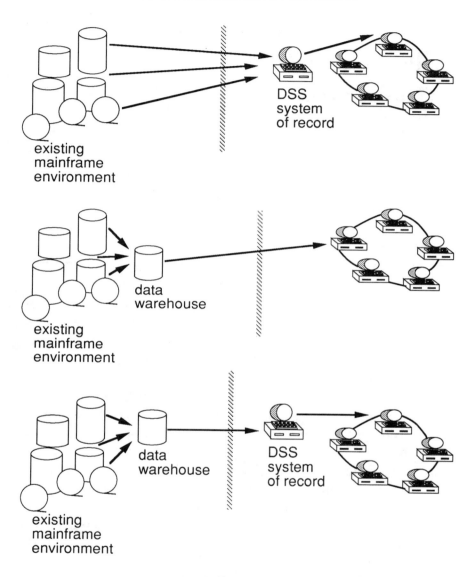

Figure Appendix.1 Getting data from the mainframe
environment to the client/server
environment.

Client/Server Glossary

access

> The operation of seeking, reading, or writing data on a storage unit.

access method

> A technique used to transfer a physical record from or to a mass storage device.

access pattern

> The general sequence in which the data structure is accessed, i.e., from tuple to tuple, from segment to segment, etc.

access time

> The time interval between the instant an instruction control unit initiates a call for data and the instant when delivery of the data is completed from the device control unit.

address

> An identification (number, name, label) for a location in which data is stored.

addressing

> The means of assigning data to storage locations, and subsequent retrieval, on the basis of the key of the data.

algorithm

> A set of statements to solve a problem in a finite number of steps.

alias

> An alternative label used to refer to a data element.

application blocking of data

> The grouping of different occurrences of the same type of data by the application programmer. The application programmer takes care of data placement, location, deletion, overflow, etc.

archival database

> A database copy saved for historical, recovery, or restoration purposes.

association

> A relationship between two entities that is represented in a data model.

atomic

> The smallest addressable unit within a system.

atomic level data

> Archival (time-variant) data at a low level of detail with a moderate probability of access positioned to serve as a foundation for DSS processing.

attribute

> A property that can assume values for entities or relationships. Entities can be assigned several attributes (e.g., a

tuple in a relation consists of values). Some systems also allow relationships to have attributes.

audit trail

Data that is available to trace activity; typically used for database transactions or for terminal activity.

availability

A measure of the reliability of a system, indicating the fraction of time when the system is available divided by the amount of time the system should be available.

B* Tree

A type of indexing algorithm used to create and store indexes.

backup

To restore the database to its state at a previous point in time. Backup is often achieved from an archival database—that is, a snapshot of the database at a specified time.

batch

Computer environment in which programs (usually long-running, sequentially oriented) exclusively access data, and user activity is not interactive.

batch environment

A sequentially dominated mode of processing; in batch, input is collected and batched for future processing throughout the day. Once collected, the batch input is transacted sequentially against one or more databases.

batch window

The time when the online system is available for batch or sequential processing. The batch window occurs during nonpeak processing hours.

bill of materials

A listing of the materials used in a manufacturing process. The structure of how the materials are used in the manufacturing process can be derived from the bill of materials.

bind

To assign a value to a data element, variable, or parameter; the attachment of a data definition to a program prior to execution of the program.

block

A basic unit of data structuring; the physical unit of transport and storage. A block contains one or more records. Sometimes called a page.

blocking

The combining of two or more physical records so that they are jointly read or written by one machine instruction.

block splitting

A data management activity that allows a fully packed block to be split into two or more blocks, where each new block contains some free space.

bridge

A connection between two rings.

B-tree

A binary storage structure and access method for use in a database that maintains its order by continually dividing the possible choices into two equal parts and re-establishing pointers to the respective sets but not allowing more than two levels of difference to exist concurrently.

buffer

An area of storage that holds data temporarily while data is being received, transmitted, read, or written. Is often used to compensate for differences in the speed or timing of devices. Buffers are used in terminals, peripheral devices, storage units, and in the CPU.

checkpoint

An identified snapshot of the database or a point at which the transitions have been frozen or are quiescent.

checkpoint/restart

A means of restarting a program at some point other than the beginning, used after a failure or interruption has occurred. Throughout an application program n checkpoints may be used at intervals; at these points records are written giving enough information about the status of the program to permit its being restarted at that point.

claimed block

A second or subsequent physical block designated to store table data when the originally allocated block has run out of space.

client

The user of data in a client/server environment.

client/server

A network environment where the control of data is established at a server node and is available for access, but not update, at other nodes.

cluster

A means of storing data from multiple tables together based on a common key value.

cluster key

The key around which the cluster is built.

code

(1) To represent data or a computer program in a form that can be accepted by a data processor. (2) To transform data so that it cannot be understood by anyone who does not have the algorithm to decode the data before its presentation.

column

A vertical table in which values are selected from the same domain. The column is named in the head.

commit

A condition issued by a group of operators or transactions when the changes to a database are concluded satisfactorily and can no longer be canceled or rolled back, except as a whole by a later special command to undo the entire group.

compaction

A technique for reducing the number of bits required for storage without destroying any information content.

concatenated index

An index over multiple columns.

connector

A symbol used to indicate that one occurrence of data has a relationship with another occurrence of data. Connectors are used in conceptual database design. Connectors can be implemented hierarchically, relationally, in an inverted fashion, or by a network.

control database

A database containing data other than that directly related to the function of the application; typical control databases are terminal databases, security databases, audit databases, tables databases, etc.; although control databases are necessary, it is mandatory that they be implemented properly.

cursor

An indicator that designates a current position relative to the ordering of the rows in a table and is open for the duration of a session.

DASD

Direct-access storage device.

data

A recording of facts, concepts, or instructions on a storage medium for communication, retrieval, and processing by automatic means and presentation as information that is understandable to humans.

data administrator

The individual who manages organizational data and is responsible for the specification, acquisition, and maintenance of the data management software and the design, validation, and security of the files or database.

data definition language (DDL) (also called a **data description language**)

The language used to define the database schema and give additional data that allows the DBMS to generate the internal tables, indexes, buffers, and storage criteria necessary for database processing.

data description language (DDL)

A language for describing data (in some software for describing the logical, not the physical, data; in other software for both).

data dictionary system

A software tool that allows the recording, storing, and processing of such metadata as data definitions, descriptions, and relationships between programs, data, and users.

data driven process

A process whose resource utilization depends on the structure and occurrences of the data being operated on. For example, a hierarchical root has on the average 2 de-

pendents but has one case where there are 1000 dependents. Any process accessing the root and all dependents
will be data-driven (i.e., behaving nicely 99 percent of the
time, and awkwardly 1 percent of the time).

data element

An attribute of an entity; a uniquely named and well-defined category of data that consists of data items and is
included in a record of an activity.

data manipulation language (DML)

A programming language that is supported by a DBMS
and used to access a database; language constructs for
addition to higher-order language (e.g., COBOL) for the
purpose of database manipulation.

data model

(1) The logical data structures, including operations and
constraints, provided by a DBMS for effective database
processing. (2) The system used for data representation
(e.g., the ERA or relational model).

DBMS (database management system)

DBMS Language Interface (DB I/O Module)

Software that applications call, which in turn calls the
DBMS. By making the interface to the DBMS indirect,
several benefits will derive, such as standards enforcement, standard error checks, and so on.

deadly embrace

The event that occurs when transaction A desires to get at
data protected by transaction B when at the same time
transaction B desires to get at data protected by transaction A. Processing comes to a halt until either A or B is
given access to data.

decompaction

> The opposite of compaction; data is stored in a compacted form but must be decompacted upon use to make sense to the user.

decryption

> The opposite of encryption; data is stored in an encrypted form and must be decrypted upon use to make sense to the user.

derived data

> Data about multiple customers or multiple events.

derived data element

> A data element that is not necessarily stored but that can be generated when needed (e.g., the age, given the date of birth and current date).

direct access

> Retrieval or storage of data by a reference to its location on a volume, rather than relative to the previously retrieved or stored data. The access mechanism goes directly to the data in question, as is normally required with on-line use of data.

direct-access storage device (DASD)

> A data storage unit on which data can be accessed directly at random without having to progress through a serial file such as tape. A disk unit is a direct-access storage device.

directory

> A table giving the relationships between items of data. Sometimes a table (index) giving the addresses of data.

disk

> DASD.

DSS data (decision support systems)

Data used in a free-form fashion to support managerial decisions.

encoding

A shortening or abbreviation of the physical representation of a data value. For example, male = M, female = F.

encryption

The transformation of data by means of an algorithm from one form to another so that the data is unrecognizable in its transformed representation; encryption is done for security reasons. Should an unauthorized person stumble on the transformed data, the data would be useless without the transformation algorithm.

entity

A person, place, event, or thing of interest to users at the highest level of abstraction.

entity-relationship diagram (ERD)

A high-level schematic of data at its highest level of abstraction.

foreign key

An attribute that is not a primary key to a relation in a relational system, but whose values are values of the primary key of another relation's tuples.

format

The arrangement or layout of data in or on a data medium (i.e., buffer) or in a program definition.

heuristics

A method of obtaining a solution through inference or trial-and-error that uses approximate methods while evaluating the progress toward an acceptable goal.

index

> The portion of the storage structure maintained to provide efficient access to a record when its index key item value is known.

instance

> A member of a shared-partition database system, as in an Oracle cluster run in MVS CICS.

interactive

> A mode of processing combining some aspects of online processing and some aspects of batch processing; in interactive processing, the user can directly interact with data over which the user has exclusive control. In addition, the user can cause sequential activity to occur on the data.

intersection data

> Data associated with the junction of two or more entities or record types but which has no meaning if associated with only one of them.

I/O (input/output)

> The means by which data is stored on DASD. I/O is measured in milliseconds while computer processing is measured in nanoseconds.

join

> An operation that takes two relations as operands and produces a new relation by concatenating the tuples and matching the corresponding columns when a stated condition holds between the two.

key

> A data item or combination of data items used to identify or locate a record instance (or other data grouping).

key, primary

> A key that is used to uniquely identify a record instance (or other data grouping).

key, secondary

> A key that does not uniquely identify a record instance; that is, more than one record instance can have the same key value.

line

> The hardware by which data flows to or from the processor; typically lines go to terminals, printers, other processors, etc.

line time

> The amount of time required for a transaction to go either from the terminal to the processor or from the processor to the terminal; typically line time is the single largest component of on-line response time.

living sample

> A representative database, typically used for analytical work in the case of a very large database. Periodically, the very large database is stripped of data so that the living sample represents a cross-section of the large database. Then statistical activity can be done against the living sample database without disturbing the large database.

load

> To insert data values into a database that was previously empty.

loading

> The automatic recording of data concerning attempts to query, load, augment, or update the database.

lockup

> The event that occurs when a database is being used exclusively and other programs desire to access the database but cannot.

magnetic tape

> The medium most closely associated with sequential processing; a large ribbon on which magnetic images are stored and retrieved.

master file

> A concept from sequential processing where a given file holds the definitive data for a given system.

message

> The data input by the user in the online environment that is used to drive a transaction, or the data that is output to the user as a result of the execution of a transaction.

MTAR (maximum transaction arrival rate)

> The peak rate at which transactions arrive for database processing.

natural join

> A join in which the redundant tuple components generated by the join are removed.

navigate

> To steer a course through a database by using such devices as indexes and pointers to arrive at and examine a record and data item values.

network

> A collection of nodes that communicate with each other.

nine's complement

> Transformation of a numeric field calculated by subtracting its value from a value greater or equal to the field consisting digitally of all nines.

node

A pc or workstation attached to a network.

node residency

The boundaries of what belongs to a node and what does not, usually mutually exclusive. A node can update data resident to it, and may not update data not resident to it.

normal forms

first normal form

Data that has been organized into two-dimensional flat files without repeating groups.

second normal form

Data that functionally depends on the entire candidate key.

third normal form

Data that has had all transitive dependencies on other data items within the record removed, except for the candidate key.

fourth normal form

Data whose candidate key is related to all data items in the record and that contains no more than one non-trivial multivalued dependency on the candidate key.

normalize

To decompose complex data structures into normal form structures.

null

An item or record for which no value currently exists or may ever exist.

numeric

A representation using only numbers and the decimal point.

on-line storage

> Storage devices, especially the storage media they contain, under the direct control of a computing system, not off-line or in a volume library.

operating system

> Software that enables a computer to supervise its own operations, automatically calling in programs, routines, language, and data, as needed for continuous throughput of different types of jobs.

operational data

> Data used to support the day-to-day operations of an organization—usually at a detailed level.

operations

> The organizational unit responsible for making the computer environment operable.

overflow

> The condition when a record (or segment) cannot be stored in its home address, that is, the storage location logically assigned to it on loading. It may be stored in a special overflow location, or in the home address of other records; the area of DASD where data is sent when collisions occur or records go when they need to be written and there is no space in primary DASD.

page fault

> A program interruption that occurs when a page that is referred to is not in main memory and has to be read in.

page-fixed

> In a virtual environment when programs or data are defined so that they cannot be removed from main storage, they are said to be page-fixed. Only a limited amount of storage can be page-fixed.

paging

In virtual storage systems, the technique of making memory appear larger than it is by transferring blocks (pages) of data or programs into that memory from external storage when they are needed.

parallel data organizations

Organizations that permit multiple-access arms to search, read, or write data simultaneously.

parallel I/O

In a nonmainframe environment, when more than one processor does I/O it is called parallel I/O.

parallel-search storage

A storage device in which one or more parts of all storage locations are queried simultaneously for a certain condition.

parameter

An elementary data item or an array of data items that specifies the data type of its values and assumes or supplies the value(s) of the corresponding argument in the call of a procedure.

parsing

The algorithm that translates syntax into meaningful machine instructions; parsing determines the meaning of the statements issued in the data manipulation language.

pc

Personal computer.

peak period

Time (day, month, etc.) when the system experiences the greatest volume of transactions or activity.

populate

To place occurrences of data values into a previously empty database. See also **load**.

precision

The degree of discrimination with which a quantity is stated. For example, a three-digit numeral discriminates among 1,000 possibilities from 000 to 999.

primary key

An item whose value uniquely identifies a record or tuple.

processor

The hardware at the center of processing; processors are divided into three categories, mainframes, minicomputers, and microcomputers.

processor cycles

The hardware internal cycles that do many functions that drive the computer, such as initiate I/O, perform logic, move data, and perform arithmetic functions.

projection

An operation that takes one relation as an operand and returns a second relation that consists of only the selected attributes columns, with duplicate rows eliminated.

purge date

The date on or after which a storage area is available to be overwritten. Used in conjunction with a file label, it is a means of protecting file data until an agreed release date is reached.

query language

A language that enables a user to interact directly with a DBMS to retrieve and possibly modify its data.

queue time

The amount of time a transaction spends after being transmitted to the processor and before going into execution; queue time is dependent on many factors: the system load, the level of integrity, the priority of the transaction, etc. Queue time can become the largest factor in poor on-line response time.

random access

To obtain data directly from any storage location regardless of its position with respect to the previously referenced information. Also called **direct access**.

random-access storage

A storage technique in which the time required to obtain information is independent of the location of the information most recently obtained. This strict definition must be qualified by the observation that we usually mean relatively random. Thus magnetic drums are relatively non-random access when compared to magnetic cores for main memory, but relatively random access when compared to magnetic tapes for file storage.

record

An aggregation of values of data items or elements.

record-at-a-time processing

Access of data a unit at a time (i.e., a record-at-a-time, a tuple-at-a-time, etc.).

record type

The category to which a record instance belongs, as defined by the record format in the database schema.

recovery

The restoration of the database to an original position or prior condition, often after major damage to the physical medium. See also **commit**.

recursion

The definition of something in terms of itself. For example, a bill of materials is usually defined in terms of itself.

relational algebra

A language providing a set of Boolean and other operators for manipulating relations.

relational calculus

A language that states the desired results of a relational database manipulation using first-order predicate calculus.

relational model

A data model allowing the expression of relationships among data elements as mathematical relations. The relation is a table of data representing occurrences of the relationship as the rows (i.e., tuples).

reorganization

Process of unloading data (in a poorly organized state) and reloading (to a well-organized state). Reorganization in some DBMS is also done to restructure the database.

repeating group

A collection of data that can occur several times within a given record occurrence.

response time (user)

The amount of time the user has to wait from the time a transaction is entered until a response is returned to him or her. Response time is a function of communication line time, processing time, and amount of processing activity.

ring

A group of directly connected nodes.

row

A nonempty sequence of values in a table and the smallest unit of data that can be stored into and erased from a table.

row id

A pseudocolumn for every row that contains the address of the row.

scope of integration

The formal English language definition of what the boundaries of the system are and are not.

secondary index

An index composed of secondary keys rather than primary keys.

secondary key

An attribute that is not the primary or ordering key but for which an index is maintained.

secondary storage

Storage facilities forming not an integral part of the computer but directly linked to and controlled by the computer (e.g., disks, magnetic tapes, etc.).

security

The protection provided to prevent unauthorized or accidental access to a database or its elements; the updating, copying, removal, or destruction of the database; or the changing or running of a proscribed application.

select

To identify a subset of stored data that meets specified criteria.

server

The "owner" of data (i.e., the node having update privileges) in a client/server environment.

set

A number of distinct objects with a membership criteria. In a network or CODASYL-type of database, a set is a named logical relationship between record types, consisting of one owner record type, one or more member record types, and a prescribed order among the instances of member records.

set-at-a-time processing

Access of data by groups of data, each member of which satisfies some selection criteria.

snapshot

A database dump or archiving of data at a given time.

sort

Arrange a file in sequence by a specified key.

SQL (see-qwell)

A language used in relational processing.

standard work unit (SWU)

The amount of processing done by a transaction in accordance with a pre-defined limit (usually measured in terms of I/O's).

subject database

(1) A database and related system designed to support business functions and their applications by managing the data for a particular subject area. (2) A collection of like data relevant to the enterprise.

syntax

The rules governing the structure of expressions or sentences in a language.

system log

An audit trail of relevant system happenings, such as transaction entries, database changes, etc.

system of record

The final authority as to the accuracy of data; by definition, the system of record is correct. There can be only one system of record.

table

A relation that consists of a set of columns with a heading and a set of rows (i.e., tuples). See also **relational model**.

transaction

> A command, message, or input record that explicitly or implicitly calls for a processing action (e.g., updating a file). A transaction is atomic with respect to recovery and concurrency.

tuple

> A group of related fields in a row of a relation; a row of the relation or table.

update

> To change values in all or selected entries, groups, or data items stored in a database; to add or delete data occurrences of their relationships.

user

> A person or process issuing commands and messages to the information system.

variable fields

> Fields that may or may not occur in a given record.

variable-length fields

> Fields that may vary in length when they occur.

view

> An external relation that consists of attributes retrieved or derived from one or more base relations joined and projected as given in the view definition.

workstation

> An individual computer, usually larger than a pc, and often customized to fit individual processing needs, such as engineering, finance, actuary, etc.

References

Data Dictionary

Durrel, W. *Data Administration: A Practical Guide to Successful Data Management*. New York: McGraw-Hill, 1985.

Narayan, Rom. *Data Dictionary: Implementation and Maintenance*. Englewood Cliffs, NJ: Prentice Hall, 1988.

Ross, R. *Data Dictionaries and Data Administration: Concepts and Practices for Data Resources Management*. New York: McGraw-Hill, 1984.

Wertz, C. *The Data Dictionary: Concepts and Uses*. Wellesley, MA: QED, 1987.

Data Warehouse

Inmon, W.H. *Building the Data Warehouse*, Wellesley, MA: QED, 1992.

Inmon, W.H. *Data Architecture: The Information Paradigm*. Wellesley, MA: QED, 1988.

Inmon, W.H. *Using DB2 to Build Decision Support Systems.* Wellesley, MA: QED, 1990.

Inmon, W.H. *Using Oracle to Build Decision Support Systems.* Wellesley, MA: QED, 1990.

Inmon, W.H. *Third Wave Processing: DSS Processing on Database Machines.* Wellesley, MA: QED, 1991.

Welch, J.D. *Providing Customized Decision Support Capabilities: Defining Architectures.* New York: Auerbach, 1990.

Welch, J.D. *Providing Customized Decision Support Capabilities: Implementation and Evaluation.* New York: Auerbach, 1990.

Design Review

Inmon, W.H. and L.J. Friedman. *Design Review Methodology for a Database Environment.* Englewood Cliffs, NJ: Prentice Hall, 1982.

Inmon, W.H. *DB2 Design Review Guidelines.* Wellesley, MA: QED, 1988.

Inmon, W.H. *Oracle Design Review Guidelines.* Wellesley, MA: QED, 1989.

Perry,, W. *Effective Methods of EDP Quality Assurance.* Wellesley, MA: QED, 1989.

Networks

Growchow, J. *SAA: A Guide to Implementing IBM's Systems Application Architecture.* Englewood Cliffs, NJ: Prentice Hall, 1990.

Hancock, B. *Designing and Implementing Ethernet Networks.* Wellesley, MA: QED, 1987.

Hancock, B. *Network Concepts and Architectures.* Wellesley, MA: QED, 1988.

Loomis, M. "Aspects of Database Design in a Distributed Network." *Data Communications* (May 1980).

Martin, James and K. Chapman. *SNA—IBM's Networking Solution*. Englewood Cliffs, NJ: Prentice Hall, 1987.

Physical Database Design

Inmon, W.H. *Dynamics of Database*. Englewood Cliffs, NJ: Prentice Hall, 1986.

Inmon, W.H. *Maximizing Performance in the DB2 Production Environment*. Wellesley, MA: QED, 1988.

Planning

Chen, P. *The Entity-Relationship Approach to Logical Database Design*. Wellesley, MA: QED, 1982.

IBM Corporation. *Business Systems Planning*. White Plains, NY: IBM Corporation, 1978.

Inmon, W.H. *Technomics: The Economics of Technology*. Homewood, IL: Dow Jones-Irwin, 1986.

Inmon, W.H. *Information Engineering for the Practitioner*. New York: Yourdon Press, 1987.

Martin, J. and C. Finklestein. *Information Engineering*. 2 New Street, Carnforth, Lancashire, England: Savant Institute, 1982.

Martin, J. *Strategic Data Planning Methodologies*. Englewood Cliffs, NJ: Prentice Hall, 1982.

Parker, M., R. Benson, and E. Trainor. *Information Economics: Linking Business Performance to Information Technology*. Englewood Cliffs, NJ: Prentice Hall, 1988.

Parker, M. and R. Benson. *Information Strategy and Economics: Linking Information Strategy to Business Performance*. Englewood Cliffs, NJ: Prentice Hall, 1989.

Yourdon, E. *Nations at Risk*. New York: Yourdon Press, 1986.

Systems Analysis

Demarco, T. *Structured Analysis and Systems Specifications*. New York: Yourdon Press, 1979.

Dickinson, B. *Developing Structured Systems: A Methodology Using Structured Techniques*. New York: Yourdon Press, 1980.

Orr, Ken *Structured Systems Development*. New York: Yourdon Press, 1978.

McMenamin, S. and J. Palmer. *Essential Systems Analysis*. New York: Yourdon Press, 1984.

Yourdon, E. *Managing the Systems Development Life Cycle*. New York: Yourdon Press, 1980.

Yourdon, E. *Design of Online Computer Systems*. New York: Yourdon Press, 1982.

Yourdon, E. *Classics in Software Engineering*. New York: Yourdon Press, 1983.

Testing

Hetzel, B. *The Complete Guide to Software Testing*. Wellesley, MA: QED, 1989.

Perry, W. *A Structured Approach to Systems Testing*. Wellesley, MA: QED, 1990.

Index